THE CRAFTSMAN'S COOKBOOK

A PUBLICATION OF THE AMERICAN CRAFTS COUNCIL

COMPILED BY LOIS MORAN

RECIPES TESTED & WRITTEN BY MALABAR BRODEUR

ISBN: 0-88321-000-2
LIBRARY OF CONGRESS CATALOG CARD NO.: 72-91347
PRINTED IN THE UNITED STATES OF AMERICA

AMERICAN CRAFTS COUNCIL
44 WEST 53 STREET
NEW YORK, N.Y. 10019

The American Crafts Council was founded in 1943 to stimulate interest in contemporary crafts. As a national membership and nonprofit organization it maintains the Museum of Contemporary Crafts in New York City and publishes the bimonthly magazine *Craft Horizons*. Through its Regional Program and Research & Education Department the Council is involved in varied educational programs including the national slide-film service "Your Portable Museum." Membership in the Council is open to all. The Council headquarters are at 44 West 53rd Street, New York, New York 10019.

Lois Moran has been on the staff of the American Crafts Council since 1963, formerly as Director of its Regional Program, and for the last six years as Director of its Research & Education Department and editor of *Outlook*, the ACC newsletter.

Malabar Brodeur has long been interested in food and cooking techniques. She attended lectures at the Cordon Bleu in Paris, and worked for three years on the staff of the Food of the World cookbook series, published by Time-Life.

Ever since joining the staff of the American Crafts Council I have journeyed into the uncommon world of the American Craftsman. As I traveled, finding myself in and out of studios and kitchens, one good meal followed another. The idea for a craftsman's cookbook had a long and tasty germination!

When the exhibition "Objects For Preparing Food" was scheduled to be shown at the Museum of Contemporary Crafts, it seemed the right time to celebrate the American Craftsman as the imaginative cook he is. And thus "The Craftsman's Cookbook" got started. Recipes were gathered by contacting many craftsmen and asking them to share their favorites with us. Each recipe was tested and proven—at least delicious and often superlative.

This book was done in salute to American craftsmen, not alone because they are so often inventive cooks, but because they are very special people. They exist in an age that is hardly dependent on them to produce the functional wares of everyday life as once the craftsman did. Yet they are indispensable to a society desperately in need of the affirmation of human values that their work and way of life fulfill.

This way of life more often than not finds them at home in charming places. Their highly personalized houses abound in stoneware and other crafts, made by themselves and fellow craftsmen. There usually is a garden—many craftsmen have green thumbs—and always a studio or workshop filled with the tools and substance of their work. There are color and warmth, not just from the surroundings but from themselves, born of a humility that makes them the friendliest of artists.

They have superb mastery of materials and techniques, most having earned advanced degrees in preparation for teaching. Some, though, are self-taught, being determined and exploring. They like to travel and to collect the crafts of this and other times. This interest and their own personal heritage account for the sophistication and ethnic variety of many of their recipes.

They assert what is most human in man—to use one's hands with spirit and grace. Long may they keep us in touch with ourselves.

Many people helped in the creation of this book—the craftsmen who gave their recipes—Malabar Brodeur—Brenda Huff who was the final check point for the accuracy of each recipe—Emil Antonucci whose sensitivity made the book aesthetically more than just another cookbook—the Council staff, especially those of the Research & Education Department and the Museum of Contemporary Crafts, and Mimi Shorr and Paul Smith—they all championed the book from its beginning.

To these and all whom we hope will delight in this book: A Joyful Sharing

Lois Moran

AN ASTERISK INDICATES THAT THE RECIPE IS
INCLUDED IN THIS BOOK AND LISTED IN THE INDEX

HORS D'OEUVRES

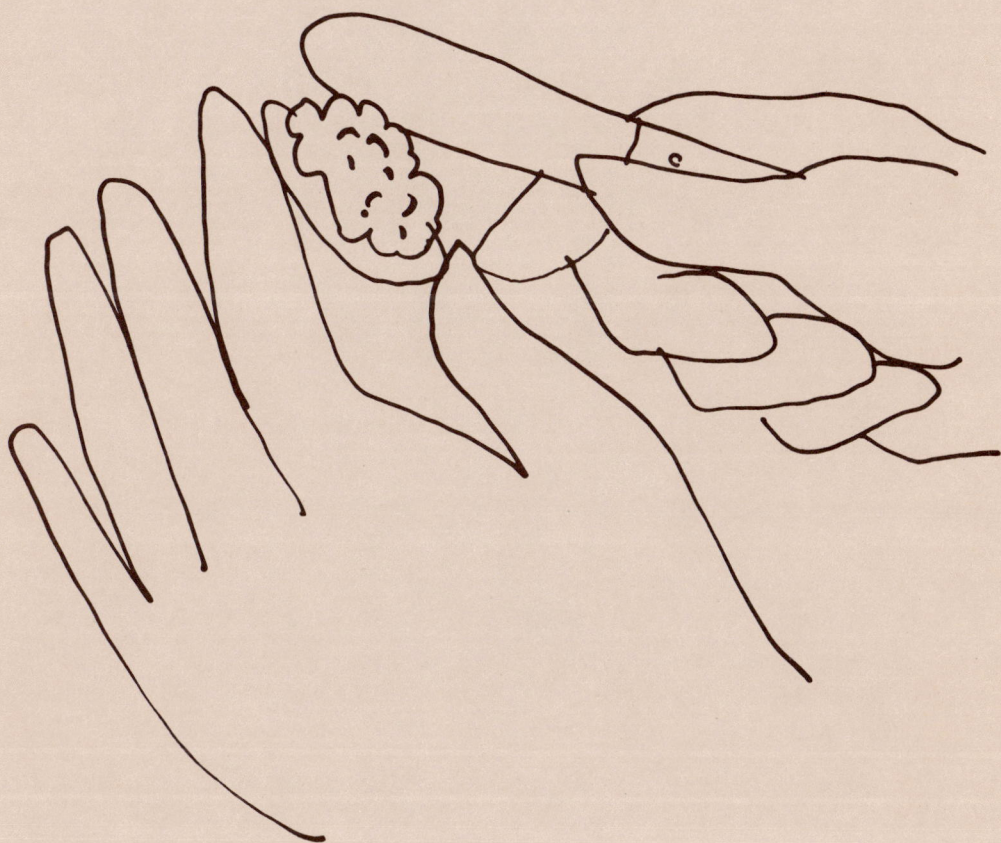

MARINATED SHRIMP
NANCY MERRITT

Marinade:
1½ teaspoons salt
  ½ teaspoon freshly ground black pepper
  ½ teaspoon sugar
  1 teaspoon paprika
  1 teaspoon finely chopped garlic
  ½ cup white tarragon vinegar
  ⅔ cup olive oil
  2 tablespoons prepared Creole mustard,
      or Dijon-style mustard
  2 teaspoons prepared Creole horseradish,
      or plain white horseradish
  ¼ cup finely chopped celery
  ¼ cup finely chopped scallions
  ¼ cup finely chopped parsley
  2 pounds cooked, shelled and deveined large shrimp

To make the marinade: Place the salt, pepper, sugar, paprika, garlic and vinegar in a pint jar and shake vigorously until the sugar and salt are dissolved. Add the oil, mustard and horseradish and shake again. Then, toss in the celery, scallions and parsley, shake, and pour over the shrimp. Stir the shrimp to coat them well with the marinade, cover with plastic wrap and refrigerate for 1 to 3 days before serving. Turn them once or twice.

Serve as an hors d'oeuvre with cocktails, presenting the shrimp in a large bowl with toothpicks, or as a first course, on individual plates, on beds of lettuce.

Serves 20 as an hors d'oeuvre.
6 to 8 as a first course.

SEVICHE

WILCKE SMITH

1 pound firm, white fish fillets, skin removed (haddock, cod, halibut)
1 to 2 cups lime juice
¼ cup finely chopped onions
2 tomatoes, peeled, seeded and coarsely chopped
1 teaspoon oregano, crushed with a mortar and pestle
¼ teaspoon ground cloves
½ teaspoon freshly ground black pepper
½ teaspoon ground coriander
¼ cup finely chopped parsley
1 tablespoon olive oil
⅛ teaspoon Tabasco
1 to 2 teaspoons seeded, finely minced hot chili peppers (optional)
1 small avocado, peeled and cut into ½-inch cubes (optional)

Place the fish fillets in the freezing compartment of your refrigerator. When they are completely frozen, cut them into ¼-inch cubes. Place the cubes in a glass or enamel bowl or baking dish and pour in just enough lime juice to cover the fish. Refrigerate for 12 hours. The acid in the lime juice will "cook" the fish and turn it opaque.

Drain the fish and wash it under cold water. Set the cubes on paper towels and pat them dry. Then, transfer the fish to a bowl, add the onions, tomatoes, oregano, cloves, pepper, coriander and parsley and toss to mix the ingredients.

In a small bowl or cup, combine the olive oil with the Tabasco and pour it over the fish. Toss again. Refrigerate for at least 1 hour.

Just before serving, if you like a slightly "hot" seviche, add some of the minced chili pepper to taste. To stretch the seviche and add a slightly different flavor, mix in the cubed avocado.

Serve as a first course on a bed of lettuce, or with cocktails on biscuits or small rounds of toast.

Serves 6 as a first course.
8 to 12 as a cocktail hors d'oeuvre.

STUFFED GRAPE LEAVES

CAROLE LYNNE LUBOVE

1 pound ground round
½ cup rice
½ teaspoon allspice
2 tablespoons finely minced onions
⅛ cup pine nuts
3 tablespoons finely chopped fresh mint
1 teaspoon salt
¼ teaspoon freshly ground black pepper
30 to 40 grape leaves, packed in brine
2 to 3 cups water
⅓ cup lemon juice
¼ cup tomato sauce

In a medium-sized bowl, combine the ground round, rice, allspice, onions, pine nuts, mint, salt and pepper and mix well with a fork or your fingers.

Meanwhile, in a large saucepan, bring 3 to 4 quarts of water to a boil. Drop in the grape leaves, stir once or twice, then turn off the heat. After 1 minute, drain the leaves and plunge them into cold water. Gently separate them, and one by one, remove them from the water. Spread them out flat on a counter or chopping block.

Shape 1 tablespoon of the meat mixture into a roll 2 inches long and ½-inch wide, then place the roll in the center of a grape leaf. Turn the top and stem ends of the leaf over the meat first, then roll lengthwise. Repeat the procedure until all the meat has been used. Arrange the stuffed grape leaves in a deep, heavy pot about 8 inches in diameter, placing the bottom layer of stuffed leaves in one direction, and covering it with another layer of stuffed leaves at right angles. Invert a plate over the top row, pour enough water over the leaves to barely reach the plate (about 2 to 3 cups), then bring it to a boil, cover the pot and simmer for 20 minutes. Pour in the lemon juice, cover, and simmer 5 minutes longer.

With a slotted spoon or spatula, carefully remove the stuffed leaves from the pot and arrange them on a serving dish. Add the tomato sauce to the liquid in the pot, bring it to a boil, and boil 2 to 3 minutes. Pour the sauce over the stuffed grape leaves and serve them immediately or at room temperature.

Yield: 30 to 40 stuffed grape leaves.

GUACAMOLE

TOM THOMASON

2 ripe avocados, peeled and quartered
¼ cup lime juice
2 to 4 tablespoons seeded, finely minced hot
  chili peppers, according to taste
2 dashes Worcestershire sauce
2 tablespoons finely chopped scallions
1 teaspoon salt
¼ teaspoon freshly ground black pepper

In a shallow serving dish, mash the avocados with a fork until they are almost smooth. Add the lime juice, chili peppers, Worcestershire sauce, scallions, salt and pepper and continue to mash and mix until the ingredients are thoroughly blended.

Serve with corn chips, as a dip.

Yield: 2 cups.

CHICKEN LIVER PÂTÉ

JODY KLEIN

½ cup butter, plus ½ cup butter, softened
¼ cup finely chopped scallions
¼ cup finely chopped shallots
1 teaspoon finely chopped garlic
1 pound chicken livers
1 teaspoon paprika
⅓ cup dry vermouth
2 teaspoons chopped dill weed,
    or ½ teaspoon dried dill weed
1½ teaspoons salt
½ teaspoon freshly ground black pepper
4 eggs, hard-boiled and coarsely chopped

In a medium-sized skillet melt ½ cup of the butter and when it foams, add the scallions, shallots and garlic and cook until they are soft, about 1 to 2 minutes. Add the chicken livers and paprika and sauté over medium heat, stirring frequently, until the livers change color, about 5 minutes. Then add the vermouth, dill weed, salt and pepper. Cover the skillet, lower the heat and cook 5 minutes, or until the interior of the livers is no longer pink.

Place half the mixture in a blender. Add ¼ cup of the softened butter and half the chopped eggs, and blend until smooth. Place in molds or crocks. Repeat the procedure with the remaining ingredients. Refrigerate.

Serve on bread or crackers, as sandwiches or canapes.

Yield: 4 cups pâté.

DANISH CHEESE MIX

MARY ANN SCHERR

1 pound bleu cheese
Two 8-ounce packages cream cheese
½ cup butter

Soften the bleu cheese, cream cheese and butter at room temperature for 2 hours. Then place them in a blender and blend until they are completely smooth. This may take as long as 5 minutes and you may have to turn off the blender several times to scrape the mixture down the sides of the container. Spoon the contents of the blender into a china crock or similar container and cover tightly with aluminum foil or plastic wrap, tied securely with string. To mellow the mixture, refrigerate it for 2 months.

Serve on crackers.

Yield: 3 cups.

GNOCCHI DI SEMOLINO

ELIZABETH WOODMAN

4 cups milk
1 cup semolina (regular style Cream of Wheat)
¼ cup butter, plus 2 teaspoons butter, softened, plus
    1 tablespoon butter
½ cup grated Parmesan cheese, plus 2 tablespoons
    grated Parmesan cheese
1 teaspoon salt

In a 2- to 3-quart saucepan bring the milk to a boil. Add the semolina very gradually so that the milk boils without interruption. Stir to keep the mixture smooth.

When the semolina is very thick and comes away from the sides of the pan as you stir (about 5 to 8 minutes), remove it from the heat. Beat in ¼ cup of butter, ½ cup of Parmesan cheese, and the salt and mix thoroughly. With one teaspoon of the softened butter, grease an 8-by-8-inch baking dish and pour the semolina mixture into it, spreading it evenly with a rubber spatula. Set aside to cool.

To bake the gnocchi: Cut 2-inch rounds out of the cooled and hardened semolina. Grease an oven-proof baking dish, or individual gnocchi dishes, with the remaining teaspoon of softened butter and arrange the rounds in the dish or dishes, overlapping the gnocchi slightly. Dot with the remaining tablespoon of butter, sprinkle with the remaining 2 tablespoons of Parmesan cheese and bake in a preheated 400° oven for 15 to 20 minutes, or until the gnocchi are golden and slightly puffed.

Yield: 15 to 18 gnocchi.

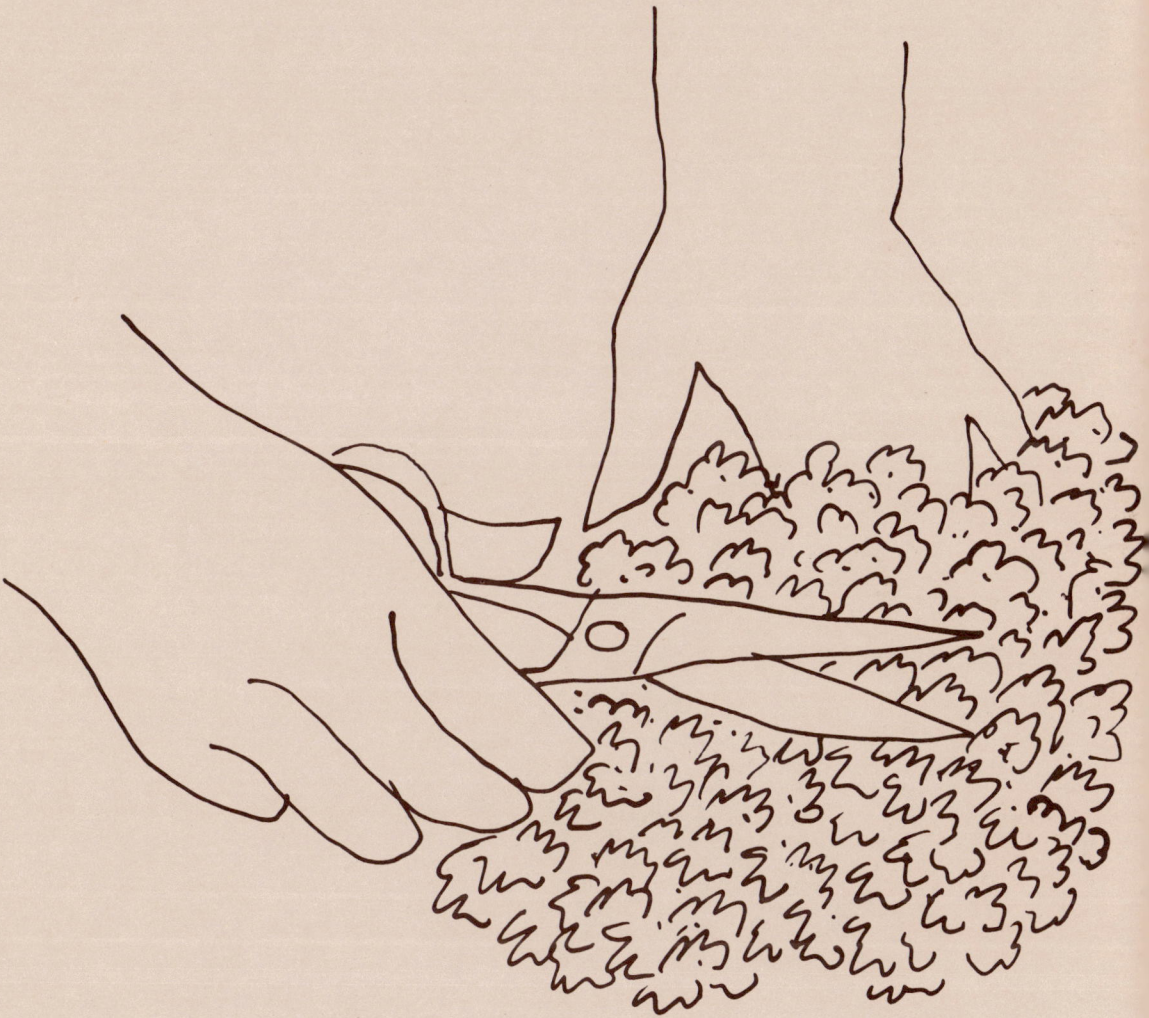

SOUPS

CARROT SOUP

NANCY MERRITT

1½ cups chicken stock
  1 cup scraped and sliced carrots
  1 large onion, peeled and sliced
  1 cup sliced celery, including the leaves
  1 teaspoon salt
  1 pinch cayenne
  ½ cup cooked white rice
  1 cup light cream

Pour ½ cup of the chicken stock into a 2- to 3-quart saucepan. Drop in the carrots, onions and celery and bring the liquid to a boil. Cover the saucepan, reduce the heat, and simmer until the vegetables are tender, about 15 to 20 minutes.

Pour the contents of the saucepan into a blender. Add the salt, cayenne, cooked rice and the remaining cup of stock. Blend at high speed until the mixture is smooth, then add the cream and blend again. Return the soup to the saucepan and reheat before serving.

Serves 4.

CHICKEN AND CORN SOUP

KA KWONG HUI

1 chicken breast
2 cups water
½ teaspoon salt
1 bay leaf
1 cup creamed-style corn
¼ cup dry sherry
1 teaspoon soy sauce
1 teaspoon sesame oil
2 eggs, beaten

Cut the chicken breast in half and place the halves in a small saucepan with the water, salt and bay leaf. Bring the liquid to a boil, cover, and simmer for 15 minutes. Remove the chicken to a plate to cool, strain the broth and reserve it. There should be at least 1½ cups of broth; if not, add water. When the chicken is cool, skin it, and remove and discard any bones. Then cut the meat into ¼-inch dice. If there is more than 1 cup of chicken meat, reserve the excess for another use.

In a 1- to 2-quart saucepan, combine the corn and 1½ cups of the chicken stock; mix and bring to a boil. Then, reduce the heat, add the reserved cup of chicken dice and cook for 10 minutes. Stir in the sherry, soy sauce and sesame oil. Remove the saucepan from the heat and add the eggs, blending them thoroughly. Serve immediately.

Serves 4.

CHILLED TOMATO SOUP

DAVID VAN DOMMELEN

One 10 ¾-ounce can condensed tomato soup
2 cups orange juice
¼ teaspoon dried oregano
1 tomato, peeled and coarsely diced

In a medium-sized bowl, carefully blend the tomato soup with the orange juice until the mixture is smooth. Add the oregano and stir once or twice. Refrigerate until ready to serve. The soup should be thoroughly chilled.

Serve in individual soup bowls or mugs and garnish each portion with diced tomato.

(For an added kick at a late brunch, an ounce of vodka can be mixed into each serving.)

Serves 4.

CHILLED YOGHURT-CUCUMBER SOUP

RUTH GINSBERG-PLACE

Two 8-ounce containers yoghurt (unflavored)
2 cups buttermilk
2 medium-sized cucumbers, peeled
2 tablespoons chopped fresh mint plus 12 whole
    mint leaves for garnish

With a large tablespoon or whisk combine the yoghurt and buttermilk and stir until they are well blended.

Split the cucumbers lengthwise in half and scrape out the seeds with the tip of a spoon. Cut the cucumbers into small dice and add them to the yoghurt-and-buttermilk mixture along with the chopped mint. Refrigerate several hours until the soup is thoroughly chilled.

Serve in individual soup bowls and float whole mint leaves on each portion.

Serves 6-8.

EASY CUCUMBER SOUP

MARY KRETSINGER

2 medium-sized cucumbers
3¼ cups chicken stock
1 tablespoon fresh dill weed
3 tablespoons butter
4 teaspoons finely chopped scallions,
    including 1 inch of their green tops
3 tablespoons flour
¼ cup dry sherry
¼ teaspoon salt
⅛ teaspoon white pepper
¼ to ½ teaspoon chicken-flavored Maggi (optional)
Lemon or cucumber slices for garnish

Wash the cucumbers but do not peel them. Split them lengthwise and scrape out the seeds with the tip of a teaspoon. Cut them in 1- to 2-inch chunks. Place half of the cucumber chunks in a blender with ¼ cup of the chicken stock and blend at high speed for 10 seconds, or until the cucumbers are finely minced but not puréed. Add the dill weed and the remaining cucumber chunks and repeat the process. Reserve.

In a 2- to 3-quart saucepan, melt the butter and then sauté the scallions until they are just soft. Add the flour and stir over medium heat for a couple of minutes to cook the flour somewhat and eliminate its raw taste. Gradually add the remaining 3 cups of chicken stock and the sherry, stirring constantly to prevent lumps from forming. Pour in the contents of the blender and bring to a simmer. Season the soup with the salt, white pepper and Maggi if you like a stronger chicken flavor.

Serve the soup hot or cold in individual bowls garnished with a slice of lemon or cucumber.

Serves 6.

KATY'S SUMMER SOUP

SALLY ADAMS

8 large ripe tomatoes, peeled and quartered
2 small onions, peeled and quartered
2 celery stalks, each broken into three pieces
2 teaspoons salt
1 teaspoon freshly ground black pepper
1 teaspoon dried basil (optional)
2 teaspoons fresh lemon juice (optional)
1 cup sour cream
2 teaspoons curry powder

Force the tomatoes, onions and celery through the coarsest hole in a food grinder. Season the mixture with the salt, pepper, and the basil, if you are using it. (If the tomatoes are not very juicy, add the lemon juice to heighten their flavor.) Refrigerate the soup for at least 24 hours before serving.

Serve in individual bowls topped with a generous dab of sour cream, flavored with the curry powder.

Serves 6.

LENTIL SOUP

EARL KRENTZIN

6 cups beef stock
2 tablespoons barley, rinsed
2 tablespoons sliced scallions
1 cup chopped celery
1 cup scraped and sliced carrots
¼ pound top round of beef, cut into ½-inch cubes
1 cup lentils, rinsed
½ pound green beans, ends removed and
      cut into 1-inch pieces
½ pound okra, ends removed
¼ cup macaroni shells
1 teaspoon salt
¼ teaspoon freshly ground black pepper
½ teaspoon dried marjoram
½ teaspoon dried oregano

In a 3- to 4-quart saucepan, bring the beef stock to a rapid boil. Drop in the barley, scallions, celery, carrots, beef cubes, lentils, green beans and okra and return the liquid to a boil. Then lower the heat and simmer, partially covered, for ½ hour. Drop in the macaroni shells and season with the salt, pepper, marjoram and oregano. Cook, partially covered, 15 minutes longer. Serve immediately or reheat for 10 minutes prior to serving, adding more stock if the soup is too thick.

Serves 6.

Editors' comments: *This recipe is very flexible in terms of ingredients. Wax beans, lima beans, spinach, even summer squash or zucchini may be substituted for the string beans, in varying quantities; however, if they are fast cooking vegetables they should be added with the macaroni shells to avoid overcooking.*

'OOSHIWALLA' CRAB SOUP

HARRIS BARRON

½ pound fresh crab meat
3 tablespoons butter
½ teaspoon Worcestershire sauce
½ teaspoon salt
⅛ teaspoon white pepper
¼ teaspoon mace
½ teaspoon monosodium glutamate
2½ cups chicken stock
1 egg yolk, beaten
½ cup heavy cream
1 tablespoon chopped fresh dill weed (optional)

Pick over the crab meat and remove any pieces of cartilage or shell.

In a 2- to 3-quart saucepan, melt the butter. Add the crab meat, Worcestershire sauce, salt, pepper, mace, monosodium glutamate and chicken stock and heat them over medium heat. Beat the egg yolk into the cream and then add the mixture gradually to the contents of the saucepan, stirring constantly. Remove the soup from the heat before it reaches the boiling point.

Serve immediately in individual soup bowls and garnish with the dill weed if you are using it.

Serves 4 to 6.

BREADS

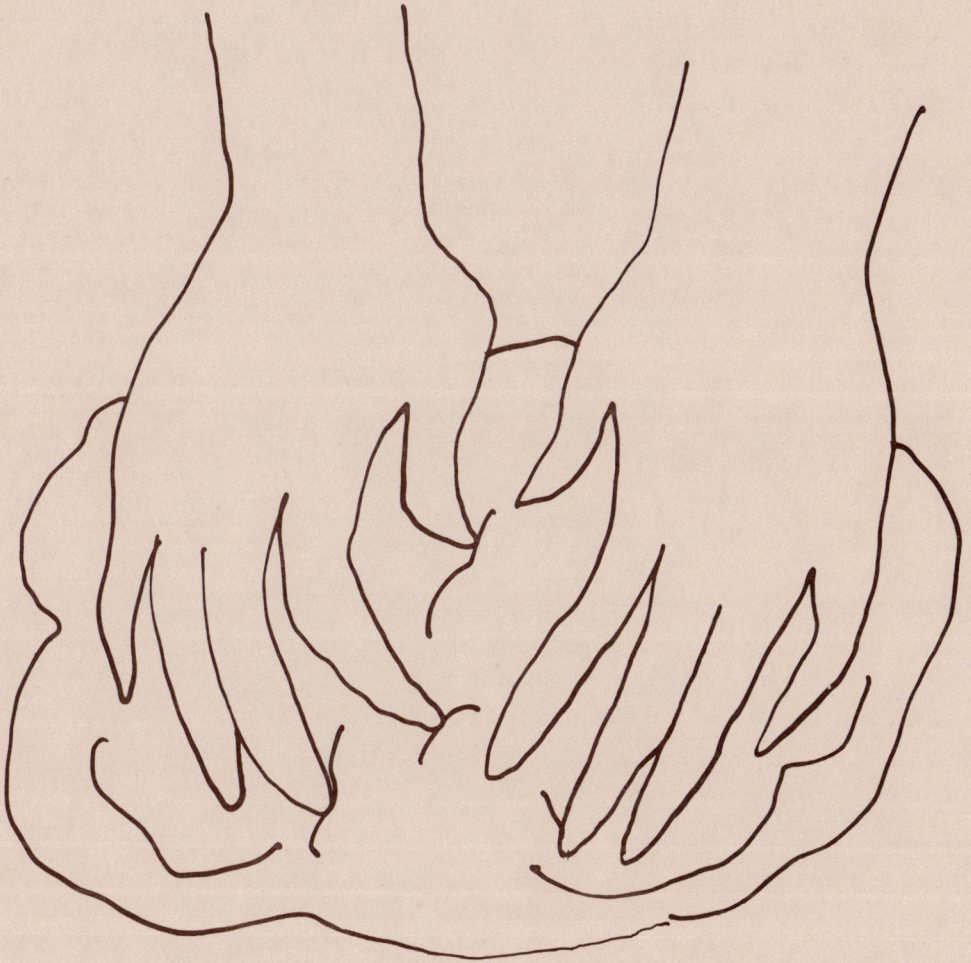

EASY OATMEAL BREAD

CYNTHIA BRINGLE

¾ cup water, plus ¼ cup lukewarm water
3 tablespoons butter, plus 1 teaspoon butter,
    softened, plus 1 teaspoon butter, melted
2 teaspoons salt
¼ cup honey
¾ cup rolled oats
1 package yeast
1 egg
2 cups flour
1 cup whole wheat flour

In a small saucepan heat ¾ cup of water, 3 tablespoons of butter, the salt and honey and stir until the butter is melted. Place the rolled oats in a large mixing bowl and pour the heated liquid over them. Stir, then cool to lukewarm.

Meanwhile, mix the yeast with the ¼ cup of lukewarm water and set it aside in a warm draft-free place for 5 to 10 minutes. If, after that period, the yeast has not started to bubble and ferment, discard it and repeat the process with another package of yeast.

When the oat mixture is lukewarm, beat the yeast and egg into it. Then add the flours, a cup at a time, and continue to beat for about 2 minutes, or 300 strokes. Grease a 9-by-5-by-3-inch loaf pan with the teaspoon of softened butter and, after dipping your fingers in flour to prevent sticking (and the dough is sticky), set the dough into the pan, spreading it into the corners and smoothing the top. Cover loosely with plastic wrap and set it in the draft-free place until it has doubled in volume. Bake in a preheated 375° oven for 45 to 50 minutes, or until the bread sounds hollow when tapped. Remove the loaf from the pan to a wire rack and while the bread is still hot brush it with the teaspoon of melted butter.

Yield: One 9 by 5 by 3 inch loaf.

HONEY-YOGHURT BREAD

SHIRLEY ECK

1 package yeast
¼ cup lukewarm water
3 tablespoons butter, plus 2 teaspoons butter, softened
One 8-ounce container yoghurt (unflavored)
¼ cup instant dried onions
¼ cup honey
2 tablespoons dill seed
1 teaspoon salt
1 egg
3 to 4 cups flour

Mix the yeast with the lukewarm water and set it aside in a warm, draft-free spot for 5 to 10 minutes. If, after that period, the yeast has not started to bubble and ferment, discard it and repeat the process with another package of yeast.

Meanwhile, in a 1- to 2-quart saucepan, melt the 3 tablespoons of butter. Add the yoghurt, dried onions, honey, dill seed and salt, and stir over low heat until the ingredients are thoroughly blended and the temperature of the mixture is slightly above body heat. A drop on the inside of your wrist will indicate whether it is too hot or too cold. If it becomes too warm, remove from the heat and cool to lukewarm.

In a large bowl, combine the yoghurt and yeast mixtures, then beat in the egg. Add 3 cups of the flour, a cup at a time, beating constantly for 5 minutes. Turn out on a board and, using as much of the remaining cup of flour as necessary, knead the dough vigorously for another 5 minutes, or until it is somewhat elastic.

Grease a large bowl with 1 teaspoon of the softened butter. Drop the dough into it, turning it so as to coat the entire surface with butter. Cover the bowl loosely with plastic wrap and set it in the draft-free place until the dough has doubled in volume, about 1 to 1½ hours. Punch the dough vigorously and set it in a 2-quart oven-proof round casserole that has been greased with the remaining teaspoon of butter. Cover loosely with plastic wrap and set it aside again until it has doubled in volume, about 45 minutes. Bake in a pre-heated 350° oven for 45 minutes, or until the bread sounds hollow when tapped. Remove from the casserole to cool on a wire rack.

Yield: 1 round loaf.

NO-KNEAD COTTAGE CHEESE BREAD

JEAN J. WILLIAMS

2 packages yeast
¼ cup lukewarm water
2 cups large curd cottage cheese
1 tablespoon honey
2 teaspoons finely chopped onions
1 tablespoon salt
½ cup wheat germ
⅓ cup unsulfured molasses
2 eggs
5 cups flour
½ teaspoon baking soda
2 tablespoons butter, softened

Mix the yeast with the ¼ cup of lukewarm water and set it aside in a warm draft-free spot for 5 to 10 minutes. If, after that period, the yeast has not started to bubble and ferment, discard it and repeat the process with another two packages of yeast.

In a 6-quart pot, combine the cottage cheese, honey, onions, salt, wheat germ and molasses and, over low heat, mix the ingredients until they are lukewarm. Remove from the heat.

Add the eggs, 1 cup of the flour, the yeast mixture, baking soda and butter and beat well. Add the remaining 4 cups of flour, a cup at a time, beating well after each addition. The dough will be very stiff, so you may want to mix the last couple of cups in with your hands, using a kneading motion within the pot itself. (Kneading, however, is not necessary in this recipe.)

Cover the pot with a towel and set it in the draft-free spot until it doubles in volume, about 1½ hours. Punch the dough down. Then place it on a lightly floured surface, knead it once or twice, then divide it into three equal portions. Shape each portion into a loaf and place it in a greased 9-by-5-by-3-inch loaf pan. Bake in a preheated 375° oven for 30 to 40 minutes, or until the bread sounds hollow when it is tapped. Remove from the pans to wire racks to cool. Brush the tops with melted butter.

Yield: Three 9 by 5 by 3 inch loaves.

EUROPEAN EGG BREAD

ELEANOR MOTY

2 packages yeast
¼ cup lukewarm water
  One 13-ounce can evaporated milk
½ cup butter, plus 3 teaspoons butter, softened
2 teaspoons salt
⅓ cup sugar
2 teaspoons grated lemon rind
3 eggs, beaten
6 cups flour
1 egg yolk, beaten with 1 teaspoon water

Mix the yeast with the ¼ cup of lukewarm water and set it aside in a warm draft-free spot for 5 to 10 minutes. If, after that period, the yeast has not started to bubble and ferment, discard it and repeat the process with another two packages of yeast.

In a small saucepan, combine ½ the evaporated milk with ½ cup of the butter, the salt and sugar. Over low heat, stir the contents of the saucepan until the dry ingredients are dissolved. Remove from the stove, add the remaining evaporated milk and cool to lukewarm.

One by one, beat the eggs into the milk mixture, then pour it into a large bowl. Add the yeast mixture, the grated lemon rind and 5 cups of the flour, one cup at a time, beating well after each addition. Turn the dough out on a floured board and, incorporating the remaining cup of flour, knead for 5 to 10 minutes until the dough is glossy and elastic. Grease another large bowl with 1 teaspoon of the softened butter. Set the dough into it, turning it once or twice so as to coat its entire surface with butter. Cover loosely with plastic wrap, and set aside in the draft-free spot until the dough has doubled in volume, about 1 to 1½ hours. Punch the dough down, turn it out on a board and divide it in half. Shape each half into a loaf and place it in a 9-by-5-by-3-inch loaf pan that has been greased with 1 teaspoon of the remaining softened butter. Brush each loaf with the yolk-and-water mixture, cover again with plastic wrap, and set aside in the draft-free spot until the loaves have doubled in volume, about 40 minutes.

Bake in a preheated 400° oven for 40 minutes, or until the bread sounds hollow when it is tapped.

Yield: Two 9 by 5 by 3 inch loaves.

REFRIGERATOR ROLLS

FRED ESCHER

1 cup milk
2 tablespoons butter, plus 2 to 3 teaspoons butter
1 teaspoon salt
¼ cup sugar
1 package yeast
¼ cup lukewarm water
1 egg, plus 1 to 2 egg yolks, beaten
4 to 4½ cups flour

In a small saucepan heat the milk, 2 tablespoons of the butter, the salt and sugar. Stir constantly until the butter is melted and the sugar and salt dissolved. Set aside to cool.

In a small bowl, mix the yeast and water together. Set the bowl aside in a warm, draft-free spot for 5 to 10 minutes. If after that period the yeast does not start to bubble and ferment, discard it and repeat the process with another package of yeast.

In a large bowl, beat the egg for 1 to 2 minutes. Add the cooled milk and the yeast mixtures and blend thoroughly. Then add 4 cups of the flour, a cup at a time, beating well after each addition. Turn the dough out onto a floured board and, using as much of the remaining ½ cup of flour as necessary, knead vigorously for 5 to 10 minutes until the dough is glossy and elastic. Grease a large bowl with 1 teaspoon of the remaining butter, set the dough in it, turning it once or twice so that its entire surface is lightly coated with butter. Cover loosely with plastic wrap and refrigerate until ready to use.

About two hours before baking, remove the required amount of dough from the refrigerator, punch it down and set it aside until it is at room temperature. Roll it out on a floured board and shape it as desired. Grease a baking sheet with 1 teaspoon of the remaining butter, set the rolls on the sheet and brush them with the beaten egg yolk. Cover the baking sheet loosely with plastic wrap and set it aside in a draft-free spot until the dough has doubled in volume, about 1 hour. Bake the rolls in a preheated 425° oven for 15 minutes, or until they are delicately browned. Serve hot. The uncooked dough may be kept in the refrigerator for as long as one week.

Yield: 16 to 18 rolls, depending on size and shape.

WHOLE WHEAT BREAD

ANN KRESTENSEN

2 packages yeast
¼ cup lukewarm water, plus 1 cup cold water
1 cup goat's milk, or 1 cup cow's milk
2 tablespoons raw sugar
¼ cup butter, plus 3 teaspoons butter, softened,
    plus 1 tablespoon butter, melted
1 tablespoon sea salt
½ cup honey
2½ cups flour
5 to 6 cups whole wheat flour

Mix the yeast with the ¼ cup of lukewarm water and set it aside in a warm draft-free spot for 5 to 10 minutes. If, after that period, the yeast has not started to bubble and ferment, discard it and repeat the process with another two packages of yeast.

Meanwhile, combine the milk, raw sugar, ¼ cup of butter, sea salt and honey in a 2-quart saucepan and warm them over low heat. When the butter has melted and the sugar and salt are dissolved, remove the pan from the stove and add the cup of cold water to the mixture. This should lower the temperature of the liquid to lukewarm. If not, allow the mixture to cool a few minutes.

In a large bowl combine the milk and yeast mixtures. Add the flour and 4 cups of the whole wheat flour, a cup at a time, beating well after each addition. Turn the dough out on a wooden board and, using as much of the remaining two cups of whole wheat flour as necessary, knead vigorously for 10 minutes or until the dough is fairly elastic. It will remain somewhat sticky.

Grease a large bowl with 1 teaspoon of the softened butter. Turn the dough about in the bowl so that its entire surface is coated with butter, then cover the bowl loosely with plastic wrap and set it aside in the warm draft-free spot until the dough has doubled in volume, about 1½ to 2 hours. (Whole wheat bread rises more slowly than white bread.) Punch the dough and knead it 2 or 3 times, then shape it into two loaves. Set each loaf in a 9-by-5-by-3-inch loaf pan that has been greased with 1 teaspoon of the remaining softened butter. Cover the pans loosely with plastic wrap and set aside again until the dough has doubled in volume once more. Bake in a preheated 400° oven for 40 to 50 minutes or until the bread is light brown. Remove from the pans to cool on wire racks, then brush the top of the loaves with the tablespoon of melted butter.

Yield: 2 loaves.

DILLY CASSEROLE BREAD

PAUL SOLDNER

1 package yeast
¼ cup lukewarm water
1 cup creamed cottage cheese, at room temperature
2 tablespoons sugar
1 tablespoon fresh dill weed
2 tablespoons finely chopped onions
1 teaspoon salt, plus a pinch of salt
¼ teaspoon baking soda
2 tablespoons butter, melted, plus 1 to 1½ teaspoons
    butter, softened
1 egg
3 to 3½ cups flour
  Coarse salt

In a small bowl, mix the yeast and water together. Set the bowl aside in a warm, draft-free spot for 5 to 10 minutes. If after that period the yeast does not start to bubble and ferment, discard it and repeat the process with another package of yeast.

In a large bowl, combine and beat together the cottage cheese, sugar, dill, onions, 1 teaspoon of the salt, baking soda and one tablespoon of the melted butter. Beat in the egg and the yeast mixture. Gradually add 3 cups of the flour, a cup at a time, beating well after each addition. Turn the dough out onto a floured board and knead for 5 to 10 minutes until it is elastic, incorporating as much of the remaining ½ cup of flour as necessary.

Grease an 8-inch oven-proof casserole with 1 teaspoon of the softened butter. Place the dough in the casserole, turning it once or twice so that its entire surface is lightly coated with butter. Cover loosely with plastic wrap and set in a draft-free spot to rise. When the dough has doubled in volume, punch it down, knead it once or twice, then shape it into a ball and return it to the casserole. (If necessary, grease the casserole with the remaining ½ teaspoon of softened butter.) Turn the dough again to grease it lightly, cover with plastic wrap and set it aside to rise again. When it has again doubled in volume, remove the plastic wrap and bake the bread in the casserole in a preheated 350° oven for 35 to 45 minutes, or until it is golden brown and sounds hollow when tapped.

Transfer the bread to a wire rack to cool and, while it is still hot, brush the top with the remaining tablespoon of melted butter and sprinkle it with coarse salt.

Yield: One 8-inch round loaf.

NEW MEXICAN CORN BREAD

WILCKE SMITH

1 teaspoon butter, softened
1 cup yellow cornmeal
½ teaspoon baking soda
¼ teaspoon salt
1 egg, beaten
¼ cup salad oil
¾ cup milk
1 cup canned creamed-style corn
2 tablespoons finely minced hot chili peppers
1 cup grated sharp cheddar cheese

Grease a 1-quart casserole or soufflé dish with the teaspoon of softened butter.

In a small bowl combine the cornmeal, baking soda and salt and set the bowl aside.

In another medium-sized bowl, combine the beaten egg, salad oil and milk, beating them until they are thoroughly blended. Pour in the creamed corn and stir. Incorporate the cornmeal mixture, mixing it well.

Pour half the batter into the prepared casserole or soufflé dish. Sprinkle the batter with 1 tablespoon of the chili peppers and ¼ cup of the grated cheese. Then, pour in the remaining batter and sprinkle with the remaining cheese and chili peppers. Bake the corn bread in a preheated 400° oven for 40 minutes, or until a knife inserted in the center of the bread comes out clean. Serve hot.

Yield: One 8-inch round corn bread.

BASIC WHITE BREAD

JEAN STAMSTA

2 packages yeast
¼ cup lukewarm water, plus 1½ cups cold water
1½ cups milk
3 tablespoons butter, plus 4 teaspoons butter, softened
3 tablespoons honey
1 tablespoon salt
8 to 10 cups flour
1 egg yolk, beaten with 1 teaspoon water

Mix the yeast with the ¼ cup of lukewarm water and set it aside in a warm, draft-free spot for 5 to 10 minutes. If, after that period, the yeast has not started to bubble and ferment, discard it and repeat the process with 2 more packages of yeast.

Meanwhile, in a 2- to 3-quart saucepan, heat the milk, 3 tablespoons of the butter, the honey and salt, stirring once or twice, until the butter melts and the salt has dissolved. Remove from the heat and cool to lukewarm.

In a large bowl, combine the cooled milk and the yeast mixtures. Add 8 cups of the flour, a cup at a time, beating well after each addition. Turn the dough out on a floured board and, incorporating as much of the remaining 2 cups of flour as necessary, knead vigorously until the dough is elastic and has a slightly glossy appearance. This will take 10 to 15 minutes.

Grease each of three 9-by-5-by-3-inch loaf pans with 1 butter, then set the dough in the bowl, turning it once or twice, to lightly coat all its surfaces with butter. Cover the bowl loosely with plastic wrap and place it in the draft-free spot until the dough has doubled in volume, about 1 or 1½ hours. Then punch the dough down, turn it out on a wooden board and knead a few more times, adding a few tablespoons of flour if the dough is sticky. Divide the dough into three equal sections, and set two of them aside. Divide the remaining section lengthwise into 3 portions and roll each into strips about 1½ inches in diameter and 15 inches long. Pinch the top of the three strips together and tightly braid the strands, tucking the ends under. Repeat the procedure twice with the remaining dough.

Grease each of three 9-by-5-by-3-inch loaf pans with 1 teaspoon of the remaining softened butter and place a braided loaf in it. Brush the tops of the three loaves

34

with the beaten egg yolk and water, cover again with plastic wrap and set aside in the draft-free spot until the dough has again doubled in volume, about 40 minutes. Bake in a preheated 400° oven for 30 minutes, or until the bread sounds hollow when tapped. Transfer to wire racks to cool.

Yield: Three 9 by 5 by 3 inch braided loaves.

EASY CHRISTMAS STOLLEN

LOUISE TODD

1 package yeast
¼ cup lukewarm water
1 cup milk
4 tablespoons butter,
    plus 3 teaspoons butter, softened,
    plus 4 tablespoons butter, melted
½ cup sugar
2 teaspoons salt
2 eggs, beaten
¼ teaspoon ground mace
¼ teaspoon ground nutmeg
7 cups flour
½ cup dark brown sugar
1 teaspoon cinnamon
½ cup coarsely chopped pecans
½ cup seedless raisins
¼ cup coarsely chopped candied pineapple
¼ cup coarsely chopped candied cherries
    Confectioners' sugar

Mix the yeast with the lukewarm water and set it aside in a warm, draft-free spot for 5 to 10 minutes. If, after that period, the yeast has not started to ferment and bubble, discard it and repeat the process with another package of yeast.

Meanwhile, in a 2- to 3-quart saucepan, heat the milk, 4 tablespoons of butter, the sugar and salt, stirring occasionally, until the butter melts and the sugar and salt dissolve. Remove from the heat and cool to lukewarm.

In a large bowl, combine the cooled milk and yeast mixtures. Add the beaten eggs, the mace and nutmeg and 6 cups of the flour, one cup at a time, beating well after each addition. Turn the dough out onto a floured board and, incorporating as much of the remaining cup of flour as necessary, knead vigorously until the dough becomes elastic and has a slightly glossy appearance.

Grease another large bowl with 1 teaspoon of the softened butter. Set the dough in the bowl, turning it once or twice to lightly coat all its surfaces with butter. Cover the bowl loosely with plastic wrap and refrigerate overnight.

When you are ready to prepare the stollen, remove the dough from the refrigerator, punch it down and divide it in half. On a floured board, roll each half into a rectangle roughly 9-by-13-by-½-inches. Brush the surfaces of the dough with 2 tablespoons of the melted butter. Combine the brown sugar and the cinnamon and mix them until they are thoroughly blended. Sprinkle the mixture evenly over the dough. Then, distribute the pecans, raisins, pineapple and cherry pieces evenly over both portions. Starting at the narrow end, roll the dough up jelly-roll fashion, turning in the ends and pinching them closed. Place each stollen in a 9-by-5-by-3-inch loaf pan that has been greased with 1 teaspoon of the remaining softened butter, cover the pans loosely with plastic wrap and set them aside in a draft-free spot until the dough has doubled in volume.

Bake the stollen in a preheated 350° oven for 45 minutes, or until they are golden and sound hollow when tapped. Lightly brush them with the remaining melted butter, transfer them to wire racks to cool, and sprinkle them generously with the confectioners' sugar.

Yield: Two 9 by 5 by 3 inch stollen

DUTCH BABIES

JACK LENOR LARSEN

2 tablespoons butter
3 eggs
½ cup flour
½ cup milk
½ teaspoon salt

Preheat the oven to 425°. Place the butter in a heavy 10-inch skillet or pan and melt it in the oven.

Meanwhile, prepare the batter: beat the eggs vigorously in a medium-sized bowl for 30 seconds, then gradually add the flour while you beat constantly. Pour in the milk and salt and mix to incorporate them thoroughly.

When the butter is melted, tip the pan to coat the bottom with it. Pour in the batter, return the pan to the oven, and bake for 20 minutes. Then lower the oven temperature to 300° and cook an additional 5 minutes. Remove the Dutch Babies from the oven, cut them into wedges, and serve immediately with maple syrup, or melted butter, a sprinkling of lemon juice and confectioners' sugar.

Serves 4.

MUESLI BREAKFAST BREAD

VICTOR SPINSKI

2 eggs
½ cup cold pressed safflower oil
½ cup raw sugar
1½ cups stone ground whole wheat flour
1 tablespoon baking powder
¾ cup skim milk
2 tablespoons lemon juice
1½ cups Muesli cereal
½ cup freshly shredded coconut
½ cup seedless raisins (optional)
1 teaspoon butter

In a large bowl, beat the eggs vigorously. Slowly add the safflower oil and raw sugar and mix until they are thoroughly blended. Combine the whole wheat flour with the baking powder and add them to the egg mixture alternately with the skim milk. Mix in the lemon juice. Then, add the Muesli cereal and the coconut and stir. Drop in the raisins if you are using them. Pour the batter into an 8-inch cast-iron skillet that has been greased with the butter and bake in a preheated 350° oven for 50 to 60 minutes, or until a knife inserted in the center of the bread comes out clean.

Yield: One 8 inch round breakfast bread

BREAKFAST MUFFINS

JEAN STAMSTA

2 eggs
2 cups milk
¼ cup salad oil
¼ cup wheat germ
½ cup brown sugar
2 tablespoons molasses
1 cup rye flour
1½ cups whole wheat flour
1 teaspoon salt
2 teaspoons baking soda
1 tablespoon baking powder
½ cup seedless raisins or other fruit
    (fresh blueberries, black raspberries, etc.,
    rinsed and thoroughly drained)
1 to 2 teaspoons butter, softened

In a large bowl beat the eggs well, then pour in the milk and oil and blend thoroughly. Add the wheat germ, brown sugar and molasses, beating well after each addition. Sift the rye and wheat flours with the salt, baking soda and baking powder and add them gradually to the batter, mixing thoroughly. Fold in the fruit. Pour into 3-inch muffin tins that have been greased with the softened butter and bake in a preheated 425° oven 15 to 20 minutes.

Yield: 16 muffins.

DUANE'S PANCAKES

JEAN STAMSTA

4 eggs
2 cups milk
3 tablespoons salad oil
1 cup Bisquick
1 cup whole wheat flour
¼ cup soy flour
¾ cup rye flour
3 tablespoons sugar
1 teaspoon baking soda
1 teaspoon vanilla

With an electric mixer, beat the eggs at medium speed. (If you are beating by hand, beat for 2 to 3 minutes.) Continue mixing while you pour in the milk and salad oil and beat until they are thoroughly blended. In another bowl, sift together the Bisquick and the whole wheat, soy and rye flours, the sugar and the baking soda. A cup at a time, add the dry ingredients to the egg-and-milk mixture, beating constantly to incorporate them thoroughly. Flavor with the vanilla.

Heat a large, heavy skillet or griddle until a drop of water dances across the surface, or heat an electric skillet to 350°. Drop the batter into the skillet by the heaping tablespoonful, spacing the pancakes so they do not run together. Cook them for 3 to 4 minutes until bubbles appear on the cakes; then turn them with a spatula and cook 1 to 2 minutes on the other side.

Serve with butter and honey or maple syrup, bacon or sausages.

Yield: 36 four-inch pancakes.

SOURDOUGH PANCAKES

RONALD PEARSON

1 cup sourdough starter
2½ cups flour
2 cups lukewarm water
2 eggs, beaten
3 tablespoons salad oil, plus ½ teaspoon salad oil
½ teaspoon salt
1½ teaspoons baking soda
¼ cup cream or buttermilk
1 pint blueberries, washed and drained (optional)

Starting the night before, place the cup of starter in a large glass or china bowl. Pour in the flour and the water and mix until it is completely smooth. Cover the bowl with a towel, place it in a draft-free spot and set aside overnight.

When you are ready to prepare the pancakes, remove 1 cup of the mixture from the bowl and place it in a glass jar with a tightly fitting lid. Refrigerate it, and use it as your new sourdough starter. It can be stored this way for several weeks, or indefinitely if you use it periodically.

To the mixture remaining in the bowl, add the eggs, 3 tablespoons of the salad oil, the salt, baking soda and cream or buttermilk. Mix well, then set aside for 10 minutes. Then, add the blueberries if you are using them.

Meanwhile, heat a griddle until a drop of water dances across the surface, or heat an electric frying pan to 390° and brush the surface with the remaining ½ teaspoon of salad oil. Pour in the batter ¼ cup at a time, spacing the pancakes so that they do not run into each other. Cook for 2 to 3 minutes, or until small bubbles form on the cakes, then turn them and cook 1 or 2 minutes longer. Serve immediately with butter and maple syrup.

Yield: About fifteen 4-inch pancakes.

Editors' comments: *The flavor and texture of sourdough pancakes, bread or rolls derives from the starter. The latter, however, can be difficult to make because its success depends on the proper blend of yeast and bacterial fermentation and this, in turn, depends on the type of flour and the amount of bacteria in the air. Either buy your starter from a bakery (many sell it) or beg a cup from a friend who already has some.*

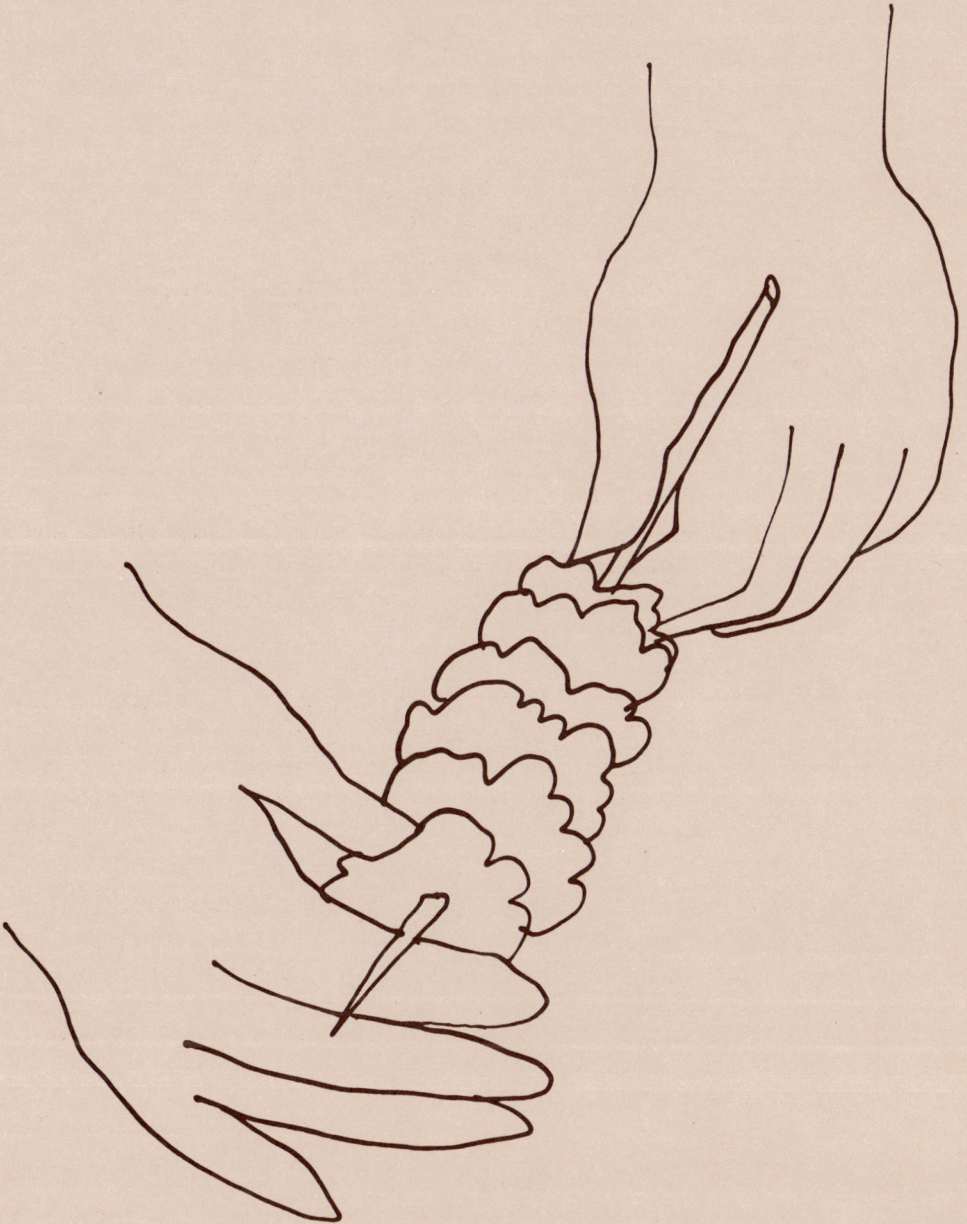

LAMB CURRY

HELEN BITAR

½ to ¾ cup salad oil
3 tablespoons garam masala or 3 tablespoons curry
    powder
1 teaspoon caraway seeds, crushed with a mortar and
    pestle
2 teaspoons ground coriander
½ teaspoon ground cumin
2 teaspoons seeded and finely chopped hot chili
    peppers
1 teaspoon turmeric
¼ teaspoon ground nutmeg
½ teaspoon ground cloves
4 cups coarsely chopped onions
1 teaspoon finely chopped garlic
3 pounds lamb shoulder, cut into 1-inch cubes
    Two 8-ounce containers yoghurt (unflavored)
¼ cup seedless raisins
4 large apples, peeled and cut into ½-inch dice
1½ teaspoons salt
    Mangos and papaya, peeled and chopped (optional)
1 tablespoon cider vinegar

In a 12- to 14-inch skillet heat just enough of the oil to
coat the bottom of the pan. Drop in the garam masala
or curry, the caraway, coriander, cumin, chili peppers,
turmeric, nutmeg and cloves. Stir for a few minutes to
develop the flavor of the spices, being careful not to
burn them.

Add the chopped onions and garlic to the contents of
the skillet and sauté them, stirring frequently, for 10
minutes. Then drop in the lamb cubes, stirring well to
coat them with the spice mixture. Cover and simmer for
1 hour.

Drain off any oil remaining in the skillet. Add the
yoghurt, raisins, apples, salt and as much chopped mango
and papaya as you like to the spice mixture. Cover and
simmer 45 minutes longer. Just before serving the curry,
blend in the cider vinegar, incorporating it thoroughly.

Serves 6.

Accompanying dishes:
Editors: white rice, lentils, Raita, condiments: chopped peanuts,
       raisins, unsweetened shredded coconut, sliced bananas, chutney,
       yoghurt.*

CURRIED LAMB AND LENTILS

KARA LANG

3 tablespoons salad oil
2 pounds lamb, cut into 1-inch cubes
1 teaspoon finely chopped garlic
½ cup finely chopped onions
1 teaspoon peeled and grated fresh ginger root, or
    ½ teaspoon ground ginger
1 teaspoon powdered fenugreek, or 1 teaspoon curry
    powder
1 tablespoon ground cumin
1 teaspoon turmeric
2 tablespoons poppy seeds, crushed with a mortar
    and pestle
2 teaspoons salt
½ teaspoon freshly ground black pepper
1 tablespoon seeded, finely minced hot chili peppers
6 cups boiling water
1-pound box lentils
3 tablespoons barley, rinsed

In a 12-to 14-inch skillet, bring the salad oil to the smoking point. Drop in the lamb cubes and brown them evenly. With a slotted spoon, transfer the lamb to a flame-proof casserole.

Reduce the heat to medium low and, in the oil remaining in the skillet, fry the garlic and onions until they are soft and translucent. Add the ginger, fenugreek, cumin, turmeric, poppy seeds, salt, pepper and chili peppers and cook for 5 minutes, stirring frequently. Transfer the mixture to the casserole. Pour 2 cups of the boiling water into the skillet and scrape up any particles that may have adhered to the bottom. Pour the contents of the skillet into the casserole.

Set the casserole over medium to high heat. Add the lentils, the remaining 4 cups of boiling water and stir well. When the water comes to a boil again, cover, and reduce the heat. Cook for ½ hour, then add the barley and mix well. Cover, and continue to simmer for 1 hour, stirring once or twice. At this point the lamb should be tender. If not, cook 30 minutes longer. Serve immediately or reheat just before serving.

Serves 8.

Editors' comments: *Curries benefit from a rest period. Thus, if you can prepare this dish in advance, it is all to the good. However, the lentils will absorb liquid even when they are not cooking, so add more water if necessary before reheating.*

Accompanying dishes:
Craftsman: rice or Japanese buckwheat noodles
Editors: chutney, Raita*

LAMB – STUFFED EGGPLANT

RUTH GINSBERG-PLACE

3 medium-sized eggplants, about 1 pound each
7 tablespoons butter
2 cups finely chopped onions
1½ pounds ground lean lamb
1 teaspoon salt
½ teaspoon freshly ground black pepper
½ teaspoon oregano
1 tablespoon chopped parsley
¾ cup tomato sauce
¾ cup freshly grated Parmesan cheese
2 tablespoons wheat germ
   boiling water

Slit the eggplants in half lengthwise. Do not cut off the stems. Leaving a ½-inch shell, carefully scoop out the pulp and reserve it.

In a large skillet, melt 2 tablespoons of the butter and cook the eggplant shells in it for 10 minutes, shifting them from side to side to cook and slightly soften the skins. Transfer the shells to a baking pan, placing them skin side down.

In the same skillet, melt 3 tablespoons of the remaining butter and sauté the onions until they are soft. Drop in the ground lamb and, stirring to break up the meat, cook until it is lightly browned.

Coarsely chop the reserved eggplant pulp and add it to the contents of the skillet. Season with the salt, pepper, oregano and parsley and stir in the tomato sauce. Cook over medium heat, stirring and turning frequently to prevent burning, until the eggplant liquid has evaporated. This will take about 20 minutes. Then mix in ½ cup of the Parmesan cheese, remove from the heat and cool.

Fill the softened eggplant shells with the ground lamb mixture. Sprinkle the remaining ¼ cup of grated Parmesan cheese over the tops, then sprinkle with the wheat germ and dot with the last 2 tablespoons of butter.

To avoid burning the shells as they bake, carefully pour ½ inch of boiling water into the baking pan. Bake the eggplant in a preheated 350° oven for 35 minutes, or until the shells are soft.

Serves 6.

Editors' comment: *This dish may be assembled hours in advance, then baked 35 minutes before serving.*

Accompanying dishes:
Craftsman: Chilled Yoghurt and Cucumber Soup*, Greek Salad*,
Stuffed Grape Leaves*
Editors: Ratatouille Niçoise*, tossed green salad

INDONESIAN LAMB SATE

PAULA GOLLHARDT

3 pounds boned leg of lamb, cut into ½-inch cubes
6 tablespoons olive oil
3 tablespoons paprika
1 cup finely chopped onions
2 teaspoons finely chopped garlic
½ cup finely chopped parsley
2 teaspoons salt

Drop the lamb cubes into a large bowl, then pour in the olive oil and toss the cubes in it to coat the lamb thoroughly. Add the paprika and toss again.
Sprinkle in the onions, garlic, parsley and salt. Mix all the ingredients well, cover the bowl with plastic wrap and refrigerate for at least 8 hours.

To cook the sate, string the lamb closely together on individual skewers. Broil the skewers 3 inches from the flame for 15 minutes, turning them four times to cook the lamb through.

Lean, boneless pork may be substituted for the lamb, but in that event you should cook the sate 5 minutes longer, or 20 minutes totally.

Serves 6 to 8.

Accompanying dishes:
Editors: Baked Tomatoes with Mushrooms* and Pilaf*

MINTED LEG OF LAMB

RAGNHILD LANGLET

A 6- to 7-pound leg of lamb, trimmed of all fat
1 teaspoon salt
¼ teaspoon freshly ground black pepper
3 tablespoons butter, softened
30 to 50 fresh mint leaves
½ cup strong coffee
1 teaspoon sugar
1 tablespoon heavy cream
½ cup dry white wine

Have your butcher trim as much fat as possible from the lamb. Rub the lamb with the salt and pepper, then smooth the softened butter as evenly as possible over all its surfaces. Cover the lamb with closely spaced mint leaves, until the top is solidly green. Wrap the mint-covered lamb tightly in heavy duty aluminum foil and bake it in a preheated 375° oven for 1 hour for a 6-pound leg, or 1¼ hours for a 7-pound leg.

Remove the lamb from the oven and raise the oven temperature to 450°. Peel off and discard the foil, mint leaves and any accumulated fat. Place the lamb in a roasting pan. Combine the coffee, sugar, cream and wine and pour it over the lamb. Return the lamb to the oven and roast it 30 minutes longer, basting every 5 minutes.

Serves 4 to 6.

Accompanying dishes:
Craftsman: Herb-sour cream potatoes, peas and salad
Editors: Mike's Potatoes*, Garden Vegetable Casserole*

STUFFED LEG OF LAMB

ELEEN AUVIL BROGAN

A 6-pound boned leg of lamb (7¼ pounds
    before boning)
1 teaspoon salt
½ cup butter, melted
2 tablespoons lemon juice
¼ teaspoon freshly ground black pepper
½ teaspoon whole rosemary

Stuffing:
3 cups bread crumbs
½ cup butter
1 cup finely chopped onions
¼ pound mushrooms, thinly sliced

1 teaspoon salt
½ teaspoon freshly ground black pepper
½ teaspoon dried sage
½ teaspoon dried whole thyme
½ teaspoon dried sweet basil
1 egg, beaten
1 large apple, peeled, cored and cut into ¼-inch dice

Pat the lamb thoroughly dry with paper towels. Trim off any excess fat. Spread it out, boned, interior side up and sprinkle it with ½ teaspoon of the salt. If the lamb appears thicker in some places, flatten it with a mallet or heavy rolling pin. The lamb should approximate a 10-by-16-inch rectangle, and be about 1 inch thick.

To make the stuffing: Place the bread crumbs in a medium-sized bowl. (They should be several days old, or toast them in a very slow oven for about 10 minutes, turning them once or twice.) Melt the ½ cup of butter in a 10-inch skillet and, when it foams, sauté the onions until they are just soft and translucent. Then, add the mushrooms and cook them over low heat until they are tender. Pour the contents of the skillet over the bread crumbs. Sprinkle the mixture with the salt, pepper, sage, thyme and basil and toss thoroughly. Add the beaten egg and stir until the bread crumbs have absorbed all the moisture. Toss in the diced apple and mix gently to distribute it evenly.

Spread the stuffing mixture on the salted surface of the lamb to within 1 inch of each of its edges. Then, starting at one of the narrow ends, roll the lamb and its stuffing jelly roll fashion, carefully tucking in any protruding stuffing. At 2-inch intervals, tie the lamb roll securely with 12-inch lengths of string. Then, with longer pieces of string, tie it lengthwise in 1 or 2 spots, as needed.

Combine the remaining ½ cup of melted butter with the lemon juice and brush the mixture onto the lamb roll. Sprinkle it with the remaining ½ teaspoon of salt, the pepper and rosemary and roast it, uncovered, in a preheated 350° oven for 1½ hours if you like pink lamb, or 15 minutes longer if you like it more well done.

Serves 6 to 8.

Accompanying dishes:
Craftsman: Steamed "Kamada" Squash*, green salad
Editors: Peas, Water Chestnuts and Mushrooms*, or Ratatouille
*   Niçoise*, green salad*

FRUITED LAMB SHANKS

PAUL SOLDNER

1 teaspoon butter
1¼ cups dried prunes
1 cup dried apricots
¼ cup flour
1 teaspoon salt
½ teaspoon freshly ground black pepper
4 lamb shanks, about 1 pound each
½ cup seedless raisins
2 tablespoons honey
2 tablespoons lemon juice
2 tablespoons cider vinegar
½ cup sugar
½ teaspoon cinnamon
½ teaspoon allspice
¼ teaspoon ground cloves

Grease a large oven-proof casserole that is equipped with a tightly fitting lid with the butter.

In a small saucepan, cover the prunes and apricots with water and bring it to a boil. Reduce the heat, and simmer, uncovered, for 10 minutes. Remove from the heat, drain and reserve the liquid. When the fruit is cool, pit the prunes, combine them with the apricots and 1 cup of the reserved liquid and set aside.

Place the flour, salt and pepper into a paper bag, then drop in the lamb shanks, one at a time, and shake the bag to lightly dust the meat with the seasoned flour. Arrange the shanks in the prepared casserole and bake them, covered, in a preheated 350° oven for 1½ hours.

Meanwhile, in a 2-quart saucepan, combine the reserved prunes and apricots with the raisins, honey, lemon juice, vinegar, sugar, cinnamon, allspice and ground cloves. Bring the liquid to a boil, reduce the heat and cook for 5 minutes, stirring occasionally. Set aside.

When the lamb shanks have baked for 1½ hours, remove them from the oven, drain off the fat that has accumulated in the casserole and pour the fruit sauce over the lamb. Cover, return the casserole to the oven and bake 30 minutes longer.

Serves 4.

Editors' comments: *This fruit sauce would be equally good with a roast loin of pork.*

Accompanying dishes:
Craftsman: rice, tossed salad
Editors: mashed potatoes or noodles, Cardamom Carrots*

BAKED LAMB SHANKS

WILLIAM WYMAN

¼ cup Worcestershire sauce
⅓ cup flour
1 teaspoon salt
½ teaspoon freshly ground black pepper
4 lamb shanks, about 1 pound each
6 tablespoons salad oil
1 cup coarsely chopped onions
1 teaspoon finely chopped garlic
1 cup coarsely chopped green peppers
1 teaspoon dried rosemary
½ teaspoon dried basil
1 cup dry red wine

Pour the Worcestershire sauce into a shallow bowl and combine the flour, salt and pepper on a paper towel. Dip the lamb shanks in the Worcestershire sauce and when all the surfaces are moistened, roll the shanks in the seasoned flour to coat them thoroughly.

In a 12-inch skillet heat 3 tablespoons of the oil over high heat and brown the lamb shanks on all sides. With a slotted spoon, or tongs, transfer them to an oven-proof casserole. In another skillet heat the remaining 3 tablespoons of oil and sauté the onions, garlic and green peppers over medium heat until they are soft. Spoon them over the shanks and sprinkle the lamb with the rosemary and basil. Finally, pour in the wine and stir to distribute it evenly.

Cover and bake in a preheated 350° oven for 1½ hours.

Serves 4.

Accompanying dishes:
Craftsman; rice, green vegetables
Editors: Mike's Potatoes*, Ratatouille Niçoise* or a green salad

BAKED STUFFED KIBBI

SAM MALOOF

Basic Kibbi Mixture:
1½ cups bulgur (cracked wheat)
 2 pounds lean leg of lamb, finely ground and chilled
 ¾ cup finely chopped onions
 2 teaspoons salt
 ½ teaspoon freshly ground black pepper

Stuffing:
 1 tablespoon butter
 1 pound shoulder lamb, including some fat and
     coarsely ground
 ¾ cup coarsely chopped onions
 3 tablespoons pine nuts
 ½ teaspoon salt
 ¼ teaspoon freshly ground black pepper
 1 teaspoon butter
 ¾ cup olive oil

To make the Basic Kibbi Mixture: Place the bulgur in
in a medium-sized bowl and cover it with at least one inch
of water. Set it aside to soak for at least 1 hour, then
drain thoroughly, squeezing it to release any remaining
liquid.

In a large bowl, combine the lamb with the bulgur,
chopped onions, salt and pepper. Knead the mixture for 3
to 4 minutes, chilling your hands in ice-water if it should
become too stiff. Then, force it through the fine holes of
a food grinder. Reserve it while you make the stuffing.

To make the stuffing: In a 10-inch skillet, melt the
tablespoon of butter, then add the coarsely ground
lamb. Stir occasionally, and when the meat is well
separated and no longer red, add the chopped onion,
pine nuts, salt and pepper. Cook for 3 to 4 minutes,
stirring well to blend the meat with the onions and pine
nuts. Remove from the heat; drain and discard any
excess fat.

Grease a 9-by-12-by-3-inch baking pan with 1 teaspoon
of butter. Then, spread one-half the Basic Kibbi Mixture
over the bottom of the pan, flattening it out with a spatul
to distribute the meat evenly. Next, spoon the stuffing
over the bottom layer and top it with the remaining Basic
Kibbi Mixture, spreading it as evenly as possible.

Run a knife around the edges of the pan, then with
the same knife, make a diamond pattern in the meat by
cutting criss-cross diagonal lines about 3 inches apart

completely through the meat to the bottom of the pan. With your finger, make a deep hole in the center of each diamond and gradually pour the olive oil into each hole and over all the Kibbi. Bake in a preheated 450° oven for 30 minutes.

Serves 6 to 8.

Accompanying dishes:
Craftsman: zucchini, Greek Salad*

ADOBO BABOY
RALPH BACERRA

4 tablespoons salad oil
4 pounds lean, boneless pork, cut into 1-inch cubes
1 teaspoon finely chopped garlic
1 cup finely chopped onions
  One 1-pound 1-ounce can Italian plum tomatoes and their liquid
  One 6-ounce can tomato paste
1 tablespoon pickling spices
2 teaspoons salt
½ teaspoon freshly ground black pepper
¼ cup cider vinegar
½ cup water

In a medium-sized skillet, heat 1 tablespoon of the oil to the smoking point. Drop in one third of the pork cubes and brown them evenly for 1 to 2 minutes. Remove them with a slotted spoon to a flame-proof casserole and reserve. Repeat the same procedure twice, using two more tablespoons of oil and the remaining pork. When all the meat is browned, heat the last tablespoon of oil, reduce the heat, and sauté the garlic and onion in it until they are soft but not brown. Add them to the casserole.

Pour the tomatoes, their liquid and the tomato paste over the meat. Then sprinkle in the pickling spices, salt and pepper. Pour in the vinegar and water, then mix well to blend the sauce thoroughly and to coat all the meat evenly. Bring the liquid to a boil, cover and reduce the heat to a simmer. Cook for 2 hours.

Serve immediately, or reheat at serving time.

Serves 6 to 8.

Accompanying dishes:
Editors: Herbed Rice*, asparagus with vinaigrette sauce and/or salad

PORK WITH APRICOTS

BYRON TEMPLE

2 tablespoons butter
2 tablespoons oil
2 pounds lean pork, cut into 1-inch cubes
¼ cup peeled and finely chopped shallots
1 cup dry white wine
1 cup beef stock
1 teaspoon ground cumin
1 tablespoon fresh dill weed, or 1 teaspoon dried dill
1 teaspoon salt
½ teaspoon freshly ground black pepper
2 tablespoons honey
1 tablespoon white wine vinegar
½ pound dried apricots, soaked in water for 2 hours,
    then drained and coarsely chopped
1 teaspoon cornstarch
1 teaspoon water

In a large skillet, heat the butter and oil to the smoking point. Brown the pork cubes on all sides, then remove them with a slotted spoon or tongs to a flame-proof casserole.

In the fat remaining in the skillet sauté the chopped shallots over low heat until they are soft, then transfer them to the casserole. Pour the wine over the meat and shallots and bring it to a boil. Continue to boil briskly for 5 minutes, then add the beef stock, cumin, dill, salt and pepper.

Combine the honey with the wine vinegar and stir to blend well. Pour the mixture into the casserole and drop in the chopped, softened apricots. Cover the casserole and simmer gently for 1 to 1¼ hours.

In a small bowl or cup, stir the cornstarch and water to make a smooth paste. Gradually add it to the liquid in the casserole, stirring until it is slightly thickened. Serve immediately, or reheat for 10 minutes before serving.

Serves 4.

Accompanying dishes:
Editors: Herbed Rice* or buttered noodles, Garden Vegetable Casserole*

PORK WITH GINGER AND SOY SAUCE

TOSHIKO TAKAEZU

Two 3-pound pork loins (preferably center cut),
  trimmed of all fat
3 garlic cloves, peeled
½ cup soy sauce
1 teaspoon monosodium glutamate
½ cup sugar
1 cup water
One 3-inch section ginger root, peeled and cut
  into ¼-inch slices

Trim as much fat off the pork as possible. Then, place the two loins in a Dutch oven with 2 cloves of the garlic and water to cover the meat. Bring the water to a boil and cook 15 minutes. Drain, discard the liquid and garlic cloves. Then, refill the pot with water to cover the meat, add the remaining clove of garlic, bring the liquid to a fresh boil, cover and simmer over low heat for 1 hour. Remove the pork from the Dutch oven and cool it. Discard the cooking liquid and garlic. When the pork has cooled, cut it into ½-inch slices.

In the Dutch oven, combine the soy sauce, monosodium glutamate, sugar, water and ginger slices. Stir over low heat until the sugar and monosodium glutamate are dissolved. Add the pork slices. Toss several times so that the pork is evenly coated with the sauce.

Bring the sauce to a boil, cover the Dutch oven, reduce the heat and cook for 30 minutes, tossing occasionally to distribute the sauce. Drain thoroughly and serve immediately.

Serves 8.

Accompanying dishes:
Craftsman: rice and a green vegetable or salad
Editors: Baked Brown Rice and Baked Tomatoes Stuffed with
  Mushrooms**

PORK KIDNEYS WITH ONIONS
ALLEN FANNIN

3 pounds pork kidneys, trimmed of all fat
½ cup butter
3 large onions, peeled, cut into wedges and separated
1 cup flour
2 teaspoons salt
½ teaspoon freshly ground black pepper
1 tablespoon dried sage

Remove their membranes, then slice each kidney in half lengthwise. Carefully cut the meat into bite-sized pieces, discarding the white tubes. Transfer the kidneys to a large bowl, cover them with water and set aside to soak for at least one hour.

In a 12- to 14-inch skillet, melt ¼ cup of the butter and sauté the onions over low heat until they are soft and translucent. In a paper bag, combine the flour, salt, pepper and sage and shake the bag to thoroughly mix the dry ingredients. Drain the kidneys and, 2 cups at a time, drop the pieces into the paper bag. Shake the bag to coat the kidneys with the seasoned flour. Then, immediately transfer them to the skillet and repeat the procedure until all the meat is dusted with flour. Add the remaining ¼ cup of butter to the contents of the skillet and stir until the butter is melted and the kidneys are no longer red.

Cover, and cook over low heat for 10 minutes, stirring occasionally. Serve immediately.

Serves 6 to 8.

Accompanying dishes:
Craftsman: grits, collard or mustard greens, corn bread
Editors: Baked Brown Rice*, sliced tomato salad

BRAISED RED CABBAGE WITH SAUSAGE
PHILLIP WARD

2 pounds ground pork sausage meat
1 medium-sized red cabbage, shredded
½ cup dark brown sugar
2 cups seedless grapes
2 teaspoons salt
¼ teaspoon freshly ground black pepper
2 tablespoons cider vinegar
¼ cup water

In a 10-inch skillet, cook the sausage meat over low heat,

stirring it frequently to break up the lumps. When the meat is lightly browned, after about 10 to 15 minutes, transfer it with a slotted spoon to drain on paper towels. Discard the fat in the skillet.

In a 6-quart enamel or stainless steel pot equipped with a tightly fitting lid, alternate layers of shredded cabbage, sausage meat, brown sugar and seedless grapes until there are three layers of each. Sprinkle in the salt and pepper, then pour in the vinegar and water. Cover tightly and cook over low heat for 1 to 1½ hours, stirring occasionally until the cabbage is wilted. Both it and the grapes will release a great deal of liquid. Serve immediately or reheat to serve later.

Serves 6.

Accompanying dishes:
Craftsman: mashed potatoes and steamed carrots

ENID'S SPARERIBS

JOLYON HOFSTED

3 pounds lean spareribs
1 teaspoon salt
¼ teaspoon freshly ground black pepper
6 very thin slices lemon
2 tablespoons finely chopped onions
1 cup unsweetened pineapple cubes, drained
¾ cup ketchup
1 tablespoon Dijon-type mustard
3 tablespoons dry white wine
2 teaspoons Worcestershire sauce
1 to 3 tablespoons dark brown sugar, according to taste
1 teaspoon finely chopped fresh mint leaves

Line a large, flat baking pan with heavy duty aluminum foil, then arrange the spareribs on it and sprinkle them with the salt and pepper. Cover the spareribs with the lemon slices, onions and pineapple cubes and bake them in a preheated 475° oven for ½ hour.

Meanwhile, make a barbecue sauce: In a small saucepan, combine the ketchup, mustard, white wine, Worcestershire sauce, sugar and mint and simmer for 15 minutes.

Remove the spareribs from the oven and drain off all the accumulated fat. Return them to the baking pan and coat them with the barbecue sauce. Lower the heat to

275° and bake 2 hours longer, basting occasionally. Serve immediately.

Serves 4.

FRIKADELLER (SWEDISH MEATBALLS)

HANS CHRISTENSEN

5 tablespoons butter
½ cup finely chopped onions, plus 2 large onions, sliced
1 pound ground round
1 pound ground lean pork
1 cup bread crumbs
3 eggs
1 tablespoon salt
½ teaspoon freshly ground black pepper
1 teaspoon ground nutmeg
1 tablespoon tomato paste
¼ cup milk
1 cup heavy cream

In a small skillet, melt 2 tablespoons of the butter and sauté the chopped onions over medium heat until they are soft and translucent.

In a large bowl, combine the ground meats, bread crumbs, eggs, salt, pepper, nutmeg and tomato paste. Scatter the sautéed onions over the mixture and blend them well. Add the milk and beat the mixture until it is smooth. Shape it into patties 1-inch thick and 3 inches in diameter.

In a 12- to 14-inch skillet, melt the remaining 3 tablespoons of butter and fry the patties over medium heat for 7 minutes on each side. Remove them to a heated platter and reserve it in a warm spot while you make the sauce.

In the fat remaining in the skillet, fry the onion slices until they are golden. Lift them out with a slotted spoon and arrange them over the meatballs. Lower the heat slightly and pour the cream into the skillet, scraping up any loose particles from the bottom. Stir until the cream is reduced by half, and thick. Pour the sauce over the frikadeller, or serve it separately in a sauceboat.

Serves 6.

Accompanying dishes:

*Craftsman: boiled potatoes, cucumber salad and lingon berries
                (cranberry sauce may be substituted)*
Editors: thick noodles, Raita*, Cranberry-Walnut Relish*

PICADILLO CUBANO

PAULA GOLLHARDT

1 pound ground round
¾ pound ground lean pork
2 teaspoons salt
½ teaspoon freshly ground black pepper
1 cup dry sherry
¼ cup olive oil
2 teaspoons finely chopped garlic
1 cup coarsely chopped onions
1 teaspoon finely seeded, chopped hot chili pepper
1 cup coarsely chopped green pepper
1 tablespoon capers, drained
½ cup ripe pitted olives, sliced
1 bay leaf
1 teaspoon ground cumin
½ teaspoon oregano
   One 6-ounce can tomato paste
½ cup seedless raisins
½ cup slivered blanched almonds

Have your butcher grind the beef and pork together
several times.

In a medium-sized bowl, combine the ground meats
with the salt and pepper. Add ½ cup of the sherry, then
toss well with a fork to mix thoroughly. As it absorbs
the sherry, the meat will lighten in texture. Set aside
for 2 hours.

In a Dutch oven or flame-proof casserole, heat the olive
oil. Add the garlic and onions and sauté over low heat
for 3 to 5 minutes, or until they are soft. Add the chili
pepper and green pepper and cook 5 minutes longer.
Stir in the capers and olives. Raise the heat slightly,
then add the meat gradually, stirring well after each
addition to incorporate it thoroughly with the vegetables.
Add the bay leaf, and sprinkle in the cumin and oregano,
then blend in the tomato paste, raisins and blanched
almonds. Cook uncovered 5 to 10 minutes, stirring
frequently until the meat is no longer red. Lower the
heat, cover, and simmer for 1 hour.

Remove from the stove and pour in the remaining ½ cup of sherry. Set aside for 5 minutes before serving.

Serves 6.

Editors' comments: *If you do not like a slightly "hot" taste, omit the chili pepper. If you like it decidedly "hot", add more.*

Accompanying dishes:
Craftsman: white rice, green salad and French bread
Editors: Red Beans and Rice*, salad

BEEF CHARBONNADE

HELEN POWER

¼ pound salt pork, cut into ¼-inch dice
3 pounds beef chuck, cut into 1½-inch cubes
2 teaspoons finely chopped garlic
3 large onions, thinly sliced
3 tablespoons flour
2 to 4 cups beer
1 teaspoon salt
¼ teaspoon freshly ground black pepper
½ teaspoon dried thyme
1 tablespoon mustard seeds
1 bay leaf
1 tablespoon red wine vinegar

In a 12- to 14-inch skillet, sauté the diced pork over medium heat until it renders its fat and the dice are golden. With a slotted spoon, remove them to drain on paper towels.

Raise the heat slightly and, in the fat remaining in the skillet, fry the beef cubes until they are evenly browned. With the slotted spoon, transfer them to a flame-proof casserole. Lower the heat again and sauté the garlic and onions until they are soft and golden. With the slotted spoon, transfer them to the casserole and scatter the reserved salt-pork dice over the meat and onions.

There should be about 3 tablespoons of fat in the skillet; if there is more, discard the excess; if there is less, add some salad oil. Sprinkle the flour over the fat and, scraping in any particles that may have adhered to the bottom of the skillet, stir and cook the flour somewhat to eliminate its raw taste. Slowly add 2 cups of the beer, blending it well so that the sauce is smooth. Season with salt, pepper, thyme and mustard seeds. Then, pour the sauce over the contents of the casserole. Add the bay leaf. If the gravy does not cover the meat, add more beer. Bring the contents of the casserole to the boiling point, then bake it, covered, in a preheated 300° oven for 2½ hours, or until the meat is tender. Check occasionally to make sure there is enough liquid; add more beer if necessary.

When the meat is done, taste for seasoning, then mix in the vinegar, blending it well. Serve immediately, or reheat at serving time.

Serves 6.

Accompanying dishes:
Craftsman: noodles with grated cheese, green salad

SPAGHETTI CARBONARA

BRUNO AND SOPHIA LAVERDIERE

1 tablespoon salt, plus 2 teaspoons salt
1 pound #10 spaghetti (vermicelli)
½ pound bacon, cut into ½-inch pieces
3 tablespoons milk
4 eggs, beaten
½ teaspoon freshly ground black pepper
¼ cup butter

Fill a 5- to 6-quart pot with water. Add 1 tablespoon of the salt and bring the water to a rapid boil. Drop in the spaghetti and stir to separate the strands. When the water returns to a boil, lower the heat, and boil 6 minutes.

Meanwhile, fry the bacon until the pieces are crisp. With a slotted spoon transfer them to paper towels to drain. Add the milk to the beaten eggs and sprinkle in the remaining 2 teaspoons of salt and the pepper. Mix well.

When the spaghetti is cooked, drain it and return it to to pot. Add the butter, stir until it has melted and then pour in the egg mixture. Stir quickly to coat all the spaghetti. Contact with the hot spaghetti will cook the eggs, so it is important to mix them in fast. Sprinkle in the bacon pieces, and serve immediately.

Serves 6.

Accompanying dishes:
Editors: Spinach and Orange Salad *

HUNGARIAN SPAGHETTI

RAY ALLEN

2 tablespoons olive oil
1 cup coarsely chopped onions
1 cup chopped green peppers
1 pound ground round
   One 2-pound 3-ounce can plum tomatoes
1 teaspoon dried basil
1 tablespoon paprika
2 teaspoons salt
½ teaspoon freshly ground black pepper
½ pound very sharp cheddar cheese, grated or
    finely diced
   Spaghetti, cooked al dente (barely tender)

In a flame-proof casserole heat the olive oil over medium heat. Add the onions and green peppers and sauté until soft, about 5 minutes. Drop in the ground round, separating it with a fork to cook it evenly. When the beef is no longer red, add the tomatoes, basil, paprika, salt and pepper and mix thoroughly. Bring the sauce to a boil, lower the flame, cover and simmer for 45 minutes. Remove the lid and simmer 15 minutes longer.

This dish can be prepared in advance to this point. When you are ready to serve the spaghetti, return the sauce to a boil, reduce the heat and gradually drop in small quantities of the cheese, stirring constantly so that the cheese melts. When all the cheese has melted serve the sauce immediately with freshly made, hot spaghetti.

Serves 6.

Accompanying dishes:
Craftsman: tossed salad, homemade bread
*Editors: Spinach Salad**

STIFADO

JANE BROWN

3 tablespoons salad oil
3 pounds beef chuck, cut into 1½-inch cubes
3 pounds small white onions, peeled
4 cloves garlic, peeled
½ cup dry red wine
1 tablespoon dark brown sugar
2 tablespoons red wine vinegar
   One 6-ounce can tomato paste
1 bay leaf
1 cinnamon stick, broken into 2 pieces
4 or 5 whole cloves

¼ teaspoon ground cumin
¼ teaspoon whole dried rosemary
1 teaspoon salt
½ teaspoon freshly ground black pepper

In a large skillet, heat the oil to the smoking point. Quickly cook the beef cubes in it and, when they are evenly browned, remove them with a slotted spoon to a flame-proof casserole. Add the onions and garlic to the casserole and mix to distribute the ingredients evenly.

In a bowl, combine the red wine, brown sugar, vinegar and tomato paste. Stir until they are thoroughly blended, then add the bay leaf, cinnamon, cloves, cumin and rosemary and pour the mixture over the contents of the casserole. Add the salt and pepper and mix well so that the meat is evenly coated. Cover the casserole, bring the liquid to a boil, then lower the heat and simmer for 2 hours, or until the meat is tender.

Serves 6.

Accompanying dishes:
Craftsman: noodles, carrots, salad
Editors: Cardamom Carrots*, Spinach and Orange Salad*

PUL KOGI (KOREAN BARBECUED MEAT)

ANNA KANG BURGESS

Marinade:
½ cup soy sauce
¼ cup salad oil
4 teaspoons toasted sesame seeds*
1 tablespoon sugar
½ teaspoon salt
½ teaspoon monosodium glutamate
   Pinch freshly ground black pepper
2 small garlic cloves, peeled and mashed
⅓ cup finely chopped scallions, including 2 inches of
      the green tops
3 pounds beef chuck, cut into 2-by-4-by-¼-inch slices

In a large bowl combine all the marinade ingredients and stir until the sugar and salt are dissolved and the mixture is completely blended. Drop in the beef slices, toss the meat to coat all the slices and set the bowl aside for 2 to 4 hours. Refrigerate the meat if you wish to marinate it longer. Turn the meat once or twice to make sure the slices are covered with the marinade.

At serving-time, preheat the broiler until it is very hot. Arrange the meat slices, flat side up in a broiling pan measuring at least 11-by-13-inches, or cook the meat in two batches. The slices may be overlapped somewhat, but they will cook better if they are flat. Broil three inches from the flame for 4 minutes. Do not turn. Serve immediately. The marinade may be used as an accompanying sauce for the rice if you are serving it.

Serves 4-6.

*See Index

BOEUF BRETONNE
MARIAN CLAYDEN

4 tablespoons butter
1 tablespoon salad oil
¼ cup flour
1 teaspoon salt
½ teaspoon freshly ground black pepper
1½ pounds beef round, cut into 1-inch cubes
1 cup chopped onions
½ pound mushrooms, thinly sliced
¼ cup freshly-brewed strong coffee
¼ cup water
½ teaspoon sugar
½ cup dry white wine or vermouth
½ to 1 teaspoon Tabasco
2 teaspoons Worcestershire sauce
½ cup sour cream

In a 12-inch skillet, heat one tablespoon of the butter and the tablespoon of oil until they foam. Drop the flour, salt and pepper into a paper bag. A handful at a time, shake the beef cubes in the seasoned flour until they are well coated. Brown them in the hot fat and transfer them with a slotted spoon to an oven-proof casserole.

As the meat is browning, melt the remaining 3 tablespoons of butter in another skillet and sauté the onions over low heat until they are soft. Add the mushrooms and cook 5 to 8 minutes until their liquid has evaporated. Mix the contents of the skillet into the beef in the casserole.

In a small bowl combine the coffee, water and sugar and stir until the sugar has dissolved. Add the white wine or vermouth, Tabasco and Worcestershire sauce and mix. Pour the liquid over the contents of the casserole, stirring to distribute the liquid evenly. Cover the casserole and cook in a preheated 350° oven for 1 to 1½ hours, or until the meat is tender. Remove from the oven and stir in the sour cream. Serve immediately.

Serves 4.

Accompanying dishes:
Craftsman: rice or thin noodles, a simple vegetable or salad
Editors: Baked Noodles*, salad

EGYPTIAN FATHIA

MARY ANN SCHERR

1 tablespoon salt, plus 2 teaspoons salt
One 8-ounce package large noodles
¼ cup butter, plus 1 tablespoon butter, softened
½ pound mushrooms, thinly sliced
1 cup small curd cottage cheese
One 8-ounce package cream cheese, softened
¼ cup sour cream
½ cup seeded, finely chopped green pepper
1½ pounds ground round
Two 8-ounce cans tomato sauce
½ teaspoon freshly ground black pepper
½ teaspoon powdered fennel
1 tablespoon finely chopped fresh mint

Fill a 6- to 8-quart saucepan with water to within 2 inches of its top, then add in the tablespoon of salt and bring it to a boil. When the water is boiling rapidly, drop in the noodles, stir once or twice to separate them, then cook them 5 minutes. Drain, cover them with cold water, and drain again. Set the noodles aside.

Meanwhile, in a 10- to 12-inch skillet, melt the ¼ cup of butter over medium heat and when it foams add the mushrooms. Stir occasionally, and cook them until most of their liquid has evaporated. In a medium-sized bowl, combine and mix well the cottage cheese, cream cheese and sour cream. Drop the mushrooms and green peppers into the cheese mixture and blend thoroughly. Set aside.

In the same 10- to 12-inch skillet, stirring it frequently to break up any lumps, cook the ground round until the meat is no longer red. Add the tomato sauce, the remaining 2 teaspoons of salt, and pepper and mix well. Remove from the heat.

With a mortar and pestle, grind the fennel and mint until the mint is crushed and the fennel has absorbed most of the mint's moisture.

To assemble the Fathia: Grease a large oven-proof casserole with the remaining tablespoon of butter, then arrange ⅓ of the noodles in the bottom of the casserole. Cover them with ⅓ of the meat mixture and top with ⅓ of the cheese-and-mushroom mixture. Sprinkle in ⅓ of the mint and fennel. Then, repeat this procedure two more times, ending with a sprinkling of mint and fennel.

Bake the casserole, covered, in a preheated 350° oven for 55 minutes, then remove the lid, and brown the top 5 minutes. Serve immediately.

Serves 8.

TIMBERLINE BEEF STEW
SHIRLEY ECK

3 tablespoons flour
1 teaspoon salt
¼ teaspoon freshly ground black pepper
½ teaspoon celery salt
½ teaspoon garlic salt
½ teaspoon ground ginger
½ teaspoon cinnamon
4 pounds beef chuck, cut into 2-inch cubes
2 tablespoons salad oil
   One 1-pound can whole tomatoes and their liquid
1 celery stalk, chopped
2 cups coarsely chopped onions
⅓ cup wine vinegar
¼ cup molasses
8 large carrots, cut into 1-inch pieces
½ cup seedless raisins

In a paper bag combine the flour, salt, pepper, celery and garlic salts, ginger and cinnamon. A handful at a time, drop in the beef cubes and toss them until they are well coated with the seasoned flour.

In a large flame-proof casserole heat the oil to the smoking point, then drop in the beef cubes and brown them on all sides. This takes about 10 minutes. Add the tomatoes and their liquid, the celery, onions, vinegar, molasses, carrots and raisins and stir to distribute evenly. Cover the casserole and simmer the stew 2½ hours, or until the beef is tender.

Serves 8.

Accompanying dishes:
Craftsman: rice, Honey-Yoghurt Bread*, salad
Editors: Baked Noodles* or boiled potatoes, salad

CHINESE BEEF AND ASPARAGUS

GWEN-LIN GOO

1 tablespoon sesame seeds, toasted* and crushed
   with a mortar and pestle
2 tablespoons cornstarch
3 tablespoons sesame oil
  A 1-pound flank steak
¾ cup water
1 clove garlic, crushed
1 tablespoon sugar
1 tablespoon soy sauce
2 tablespoons butter
½ pound mushrooms, thinly sliced
1 pound asparagus, tough ends removed and
   sliced diagonally into 1½-inch pieces
¼ teaspoon monosodium glutamate
½ teaspoon salt
¼ teaspoon freshly ground black pepper
1 tablespoon thinly sliced scallions

In a small bowl combine the crushed sesame seeds, 1 tablespoon of the cornstarch and 1 tablespoon of sesame oil and, with the back of a spoon, mash them to a well-blended paste. Rub the mixture into both sides of the flank steak. Cut the beef lengthwise into three long strips and, holding the knife at a 45° angle, cut each strip into slices ¼-inch thick. Set aside at room temperature for at least one hour.

When you are ready to serve the meal, make sure that all the ingredients are prepared and close at hand. Mix the remaining tablespoon of cornstarch with ¼ cup of the water and blend until the cornstarch is dissolved. This dish is cooked by the stir-fried method and once you start, there's no stopping!

In a 10- to 12-inch skillet, heat the remaining 2 tablespoons of sesame oil over a medium-to-high flame. Drop in the crushed garlic and the meat. Sprinkle with the sugar and soy sauce. Toss rapidly until the meat barely turns color. Be careful not to overcook. Remove the beef to a platter and reserve.

Melt the butter in the same skillet and drop in the mushrooms. Stir for a minute or two, then add the remaining ½ cup of water. Cook for 2 to 3 minutes, turning and stirring so that all the mushrooms simmer evenly. When they have become slightly transparent, add the sliced asparagus. Mix well, cover, lower the heat and simmer for 5 to 6 minutes. The asparagus should still be bright green but tender. Return the meat to the skillet and sprinkle it with the monosodium glutamate, salt and pepper. Then add the cornstarch and water mixture and, stirring constantly, cook 2 to 3 minutes longer, or until the sauce thickens and the beef is heated throughout. Scatter the scallions over the beef and asparagus and serve immediately.

Serves 2-3.

Accompanying dishes:
Craftsman: Cha Sew Duck
Editors: rice

*See Index

ALWAYS RARE ROASt BEEF

MARY BALZER BVSKIRK

A 3- to 8-pound beef roast
freshly ground black pepper
salt

Place the beef in a roasting pan and sprinkle it generously with pepper. As salt extracts juices, salt it only after it is cooked.

Preheat the oven to 500° and cook the roast 5 minutes per pound of meat. Then turn the oven off, but do not open it. The roast must remain in the gradually diminishing heat for a total of 1 hour per pound. It can stay in the oven as long as you like, but it *must* remain there the prescribed amount of time. A 3-pound roast *must* cook a total of 3 hours, with the oven at 500° for the first 15 minutes. If you have an 8-pound roast, it *must* stay in the oven a total of 8 hours, with the oven at 500° for the first 40 minutes.

Editors' comments: *This is an interesting way to prepare roast beef. Although it will never supplant the traditional method, it offers great cooking convenience and peace of mind and is a valuable recipe for these reasons.*

The recipe is ideal when you can't be sure of your serving-time. The beef will be warm, but not hot; it will be juicy, but not dripping "blood gravy"; it will ALWAYS be rare, no matter when you take it out of the oven.

Accompanying dishes:
Craftsman: Yorkshire pudding (prepared after roast has been removed from the oven), green vegetable

BOILED BRISKET OF BEEF

JUDI MEYERS HALEM

1 teaspoon salt
½ teaspoon freshly ground black pepper
   A 3-pound brisket of beef
   One 1-pound can tomatoes and their liquid
   Boiling water
4 cloves garlic, peeled
1 cup thinly sliced onions
8 small white onions, peeled
1 whole, scraped carrot, plus 4 carrots, scraped and halved
5 to 6 celery stalks, including their leaves
1 teaspoon dried basil
2 bay leaves
1 teaspoon dried thyme
8 new potatoes, unpeeled (about 1 pound)
½ pound string beans, ends removed

Rub the salt and pepper into the fatty sides of the beef. Brown the meat 5 minutes on each side in a very hot skillet, or at 400° in an electric skillet. (Because of the fat on the brisket, no additional oil is necessary.) Transfer the beef to a flame-proof casserole or a Dutch oven. Add the tomatoes and their juices, then pour boiling water into the casserole until the liquid is level with the meat.

Drop in the garlic, sliced onions, small white onions, the whole carrot, celery stalks, basil, bay leaves and thyme. Bring the liquid to a boil, reduce the heat and simmer, covered, for 2½ hours.

With a slotted spoon, remove and discard the celery stalks and carrot. Drop in the new potatoes and cook, uncovered, over low heat for ½ hour. Then add the remaining carrot halves and the string beans, lower the heat, and simmer, covered, for 15 minutes.

Serve the brisket, sliced, in shallow soup bowls with an assortment of the vegetables and a generous spoonful of the broth. Horseradish sauce or French mustard enhances the flavor.

Serves 6.

Accompanying dishes:
Craftsman: green salad
*Editors: Salade Diable**

TWO CRAFTSMEN'S SAUERBRATEN

CYNTHIA SCHIRA

MARILYN PAPPAS

Marinade:
   3 cups cider vinegar
   1 cup water
   4 teaspoons pickling spices
   8 large prunes
   2 medium-sized onions, thinly sliced
     A 4- to 5-pound bottom round roast
   2 tablespoons butter
   1 cup coarsely chopped onions
   ¼ teaspoon paprika
   1 teaspoon sugar
     One 1-pound 1-ounce can Italian plum tomatoes, chopped with their liquid reserved
   1 small carrot, scraped and finely chopped
   6 ginger snaps, crushed
   3 tablespoons salad oil
   ¼ cup flour
   ¼ cup sour cream

In a 2-quart saucepan, combine the vinegar, water, pickling spices, prunes and sliced onions. Bring the liquid to a boil and cook for 2 minutes. Cool.

Place the beef in a large enamel or earthenware dish, and pour the marinade over it. Refrigerate for 3 or 4 days, turning the meat once or twice each day to distribute the marinade evenly.

To make the sauerbraten: Lift the beef out of the marinade and wipe it with a damp cloth. Strain the marinade and reserve the liquid; discard the onions and prunes.

In a medium-sized skillet, melt the butter. When it foams, add the chopped onions and sauté them until they are soft. Then add the paprika, sugar, chopped tomatoes and their liquid, the carrot, and ginger snaps. Cook for 1 to 2 minutes, then remove from the heat.

Meanwhile, in a large Dutch oven or flame-proof casserole, heat the oil to the smoking point. Dust the beef with the flour, then brown it evenly in the oil. Add the contents of the skillet to the Dutch oven or casserole and enough of the strained marinade to reach halfway up the meat, about 1 to 1½ cups. Mix well, then bring the liquid to a boil, cover the casserole or Dutch oven and place in a preheated 350° oven for 2 to 2½ hours, or until the meat is tender.

Remove the beef to a heated platter. Skim off any fat on the surface of the liquid, then place the liquid in a blender and blend until smooth. Pour it into a 2-quart saucepan and reheat it, beating in the sour cream. Serve immediately with part of the sauce poured over the meat, and the remainder served in a sauceboat.

Serves 6 to 8.

Editors' comment: *In trying to avoid duplicate dishes and, at the same time, offer as much variety as possible within limited space, two intriguing recipes for sauerbraten were combined with a delectable result.*

Accompanying dishes:
Cynthia Schira: Potato Dumplings*, tossed green salad
Marilyn Pappas: Noodles and applesauce

CABBAGE AND CARROT BORSCHT

W. RON CROSIER

2 tablespoons olive oil
1 pound soup bones
   A 3-pound beef pot roast
1 large onion, peeled and quartered
8 celery stalks (including the leaves) cut into halves
5 or 6 large parsley sprigs
1 bay leaf
1 tablespoon salt
½ teaspoon freshly ground black pepper
2 cups scraped and sliced carrots
6 cups shredded green cabbage
1 large boiling potato, peeled
2 tablespoons sugar
2 tablespoons lemon juice
3 tablespoons tomato paste

¼ **cup dry sherry**
   sour cream
   freshly chopped dill weed

In a 12-inch skillet heat the oil to the smoking point and brown the soup bones and pot roast. Remove them with a slotted spoon to a flame-proof casserole just large enough to hold the beef and bones.

Drop in the quartered onion, celery stalks, parsley, bay leaf, salt and pepper. Then pour in enough water to barely cover the beef, bring it to a boil, cover, reduce the heat and simmer undisturbed for 2 hours.

Pick out and discard the soup bones and transfer the roast to a board. Cut the beef into bite-size chunks and reserve them. Strain the broth and discard the vegetables. Skim off as much fat from the broth as possible or, if you have the time, refrigerate it to congeal the fat and facilitate its removal.

Return the broth to the casserole and drop in the beef chunks, carrots, cabbage and potato. Thoroughly mix in the sugar, lemon juice, tomato paste and sherry. Bring the liquid to a boil, partially cover the casserole, then reduce the heat and simmer 1 hour longer.

With a slotted spoon, remove the potato from the broth and mash it. Return the mashed potato to the casserole, stirring once or twice.

The borscht may be brought to the table at this point, or it can be cooled and reheated at serving time. Present it in individual soup bowls and garnish with the sour cream and dill weed.

Serves 6 to 8.

Editors' comment: *While this is technically a soup, it may be served as a hearty main course.*

Accompanying dishes:
Craftsman: black bread, green salad
*Editors: Salade Diable**

POT ROAST, HAWAIIAN STYLE

JEAN J. WILLIAMS

A 3- to 4-pound chuck roast
2 cups coarsely chopped onions
4 cups coarsely chopped green peppers
1 teaspoon peeled and grated fresh ginger root
1 teaspoon finely chopped garlic
½ cup soy sauce
2 tablespoons cornstarch

Place the chuck roast in a large, oven-proof casserole, scatter the onions, peppers, ginger and garlic around it and pour the soy sauce over it. Cover and, basting occasionally, cook in a preheated 300° oven for 2½ to 3 hours until the beef is tender.

When the meat is done, remove it to a heated platter. Strain the broth into a 1-quart saucepan, reserving the cooked vegetables. Carefully skim as much fat as possible from the surface of the broth. In a small bowl combine ½ cup of the broth with the cornstarch and mix thoroughly until the liquid is smooth. Heat the broth and gradually pour in the cornstarch mixture, stirring constantly as it thickens. Return the vegetables to the gravy and reheat them.

To serve, pour a cup or so of the gravy over the meat and present the rest in a gravy boat with the pot roast.

Serves 6 to 8.

Accompanying dishes:
Craftsman: To be traditional, it should be served with rice
Editors: Baked Brown Rice*, or noodles, or potatoes, Honeyed
Carrots with Cashews*, or Spinach and Orange Salad*

STIR-FRIED STEAK IN WINE

PAULA WINOKUR

¼ cup soy sauce
1 cup dry white wine
4 teaspoons cornstarch
1 tablespoon sugar
1 teaspoon peeled and grated fresh ginger root (optional)
1 pound round steak, cut diagonally into ¼-inch slices
¼ cup salad oil
1 cup thinly sliced celery
½ pound mushrooms, thinly sliced
1 cup thinly sliced water chestnuts

In a medium-sized bowl combine the soy sauce, white wine, cornstarch and sugar and stir until the cornstarch and sugar are thoroughly dissolved. If you are using it, add the grated fresh ginger root. Drop in the beef slices, stirring to make certain all the meat is covered by the soy sauce mixture. Marinate in the refrigerator for at least 30 minutes.

Shortly before you are ready to serve dinner, heat the oil in a 12-inch skillet over a high flame. Add the celery, mushrooms and water chestnuts and cook, stirring frequently, for 2 minutes. Drop in the beef slices and their marinade and mix well. Cook 2 minutes longer, stirring continually, then cover the skillet, lower the flame, and simmer a few minutes longer until the sauce thickens. Do not overcook: Vegetables in a Chinese dish should always retain their color and crispness. Serve immediately.

Serves 4.

Accompanying dishes:
Craftsman: rice, French bread, lettuce and sunflower-seed salad
*Editors: Baked Tomatoes Stuffed with Mushrooms**

VEAL SCALOPPINE WITH MUSHROOMS AND CHEESE

MARY NYBURG

½ cup butter
2 pounds veal for scaloppine, sliced and pounded very thin
½ pound mushrooms, thinly sliced
¼ cup dry sherry

Sauce:
1 tablespoon butter
1 tablespoon flour
½ cup chicken stock
½ cup milk
1 egg yolk
Pinch of nutmeg
½ teaspoon salt
Pinch of white pepper
½ pound Swiss cheese, coarsely grated

In a 12- to 14-inch skillet melt the butter until it foams. Over a high flame sear the veal slices 30 seconds on each side. (Do not overcook. It is very important that the meat merely be lightly browned as veal toughens readily and further cooking is called for at a later stage in the recipe.) As the veal is done, remove it to an oven-proof baking dish large enough to accommodate the slices in one layer.

In the butter remaining in the skillet, sauté the mushrooms for 5 minutes, or until they just turn color. Then arrange them over the veal. Pour the sherry into the skillet, bring it to a boil and with a wooden spoon, scrape in all the particles that cling to the skillet. Pour these juices over the veal and mushrooms.

To make the sauce: In a small saucepan melt the tablespoon of butter and the flour. Stir rapidly for 1 or 2 minutes to cook the flour somewhat and eliminate its raw taste. Gradually pour in the chicken stock and milk, stirring constantly so that no lumps form. When the sauce has thickened, remove it from the heat, and beat in the egg yolk. Add the nutmeg, salt and white pepper, and pour the sauce over the veal and mushrooms, distributing it as evenly as possible. Sprinkle the top with the grated Swiss cheese.

(At this point the dish can be set aside—at room temperature or in the refrigerator, depending upon the length of time involved—until its final preparation.) Place the veal in a preheated 425° oven and bake for 15 minutes if it has been refrigerated, or 10 minutes if it has been kept at room temperature. When the sauce begins to bubble and melt place the baking dish under the broiler for 5 minutes to brown the cheese. Serve immediately.

Serves 6.

Accompanying dishes:
Craftsman: spaghetti with garlic butter, green salad, and fruit
Editors: Ratatouille Niçoise*, Spinach and Orange Salad*

CHINESE ROAST DUCK WITH PLUM SAUCE

ALICE PARROTT

A 5- to 6-pound duck
2 cups seedless grapes
2 cups finely chopped celery
½ teaspoon salt
½ teaspoon monosodium glutamate
1 tablespoon orange marmalade
1 tablespoon orange liqueur,
    such as Cointreau or Grand Marnier

Plum Sauce:
1 cup plum sauce (available at Chinese grocery stores)
1 teaspoon grated onion
1 tablespoon red wine vinegar
½ teaspoon allspice
¼ teaspoon ground ginger

Clean and dry the duck's cavity. Combine the grapes and celery and fill the cavity with the mixture, then sew it up. Sprinkle the skin with the salt and monosodium glutamate. Bake the duck in a preheated 150° oven for 8 to 10 hours, or overnight. The duck will barely cook and it will render most of its fat. Remove it from the oven and pour off and discard all the fat. If you are not cooking the duck immediately, refrigerate it until 2 hours before serving-time.

One hour before serving, cover the skin of the duck with the orange marmalade. Bake the duck in a preheated 350° oven for 45 minutes to 1 hour, until the skin is dark brown and very shiny. Just before removing it from the oven, sprinkle it with the orange liqueur, then transfer it to a heated platter and serve immediately with the Plum Sauce on the side.

To make the Plum Sauce: Combine the plum sauce, grated onion, vinegar, allspice and ground ginger in a small saucepan and simmer for 15 minutes, stirring occasionally.

Serves 2 to 3.

Accompanying dishes:
Craftsman: a green vegetable, salad, and brown rice
Editors: mashed potatoes, Spinach Salad*

'CHINESE' TURKEY

ROBERT EBENDORF

A 10- to 18-pound turkey
6 cups water
1½ cups soy sauce
1 cup dry sherry
4 scallions, peeled and trimmed
Three ¼-inch slices peeled ginger root
1 teaspoon salt
2 to 3 apples, halved
6 to 8 celery stalks, including their leaves

In a Dutch oven or a pan large enough to accommodate the turkey, combine the water, soy sauce, sherry, scallions, ginger and salt. Bring the mixture to a boil and stir until the salt is dissolved.

Meanwhile, place the halved apples and the celery stalks in the turkey cavity and sew it up tightly, then truss the bird securely.

Gently lower the turkey into the boiling broth, cover and simmer it 5 minutes per pound of turkey. Turn it every 15 minutes, so that all sides of the turkey are eventually immersed in the liquid.

Transfer the turkey to a roasting pan and reserve its cooking liquid. Baste it with 1 cup of the broth, then bake it in a preheated 350° oven 9 minutes per pound of turkey. Baste it every 15 minutes with ½ cup of the reserved liquid. The turkey is cooked when the drumstick meat is tender and its juices run clear.

By this method a 10-pound turkey cooks 50 minutes on top of the stove and 90 minutes in the oven; an 18-pound turkey cooks 1½ hours on top of the stove and 2¾ hours in the oven.

Accompanying dishes:
Craftsman: "The whole Thanksgiving layout!"

GAME HEN WITH ALMONDS

MAIJA WOOF PEEPLES

1 cup almonds, ground in a blender
2 teaspoons salt
½ teaspoon white pepper
1 teaspoon mixed salad herbs
3 Rock Cornish game hens, quartered
2 tablespoons salad oil
7 tablespoons butter
1 pound mushrooms, thinly sliced
   One 6-ounce can water chestnuts, drained and
      sliced
1 cup dry white wine

In a paper bag, combine the ground almonds, 1 teaspoon of the salt, the pepper and salad herbs, then shake the bag to thoroughly mix the ingredients. Drop 4 pieces of the hen into the bag and shake vigorously to coat the hen with the almond mixture. Repeat the procedure twice more with the remaining pieces.

In a 10- to 12-inch skillet, heat the oil and 2 tablespoons of the butter until they foam. Over medium heat, sauté 4 quarters of the hen at a time until they are golden brown on all sides. With a slotted spoon or tongs, transfer them to an oven-proof casserole.

In another large skillet, melt the 5 remaining tablespoons of butter until it foams. Sauté the mushrooms in the butter, stirring frequently, until their liquid has evaporated. Transfer them to the casserole, then add the sliced water chestnuts and the remaining teaspoon of salt. Pour the wine over the contents of the casserole. Cover, and bake in a preheated 350° oven for 20 minutes. Remove the lid, baste with the casserole juices, and cook, uncovered, 10 minutes longer.

Serves 6.

Accompanying dishes:
Craftsman: rice, tossed green salad
Editors: Bulgur with Broccoli and Tomatoes*, green salad

CHICKEN OREGANATO

JAMIE BENNETT

Marinade:
- ⅓ cup salad oil
- ¼ cup lemon juice
- 2 tablespoons finely chopped parsley
- 2 teaspoons oregano
- 1 teaspoon finely chopped garlic
- 1 teaspoon salt
- ¼ teaspoon freshly ground black pepper
- A 3-pound chicken, cut into eight pieces

In a large mixing bowl, combine the oil, lemon juice, parsley, oregano, garlic, salt and pepper, and mix until the salt is dissolved. Drop in the chicken pieces and toss to coat them evenly with the marinade. Refrigerate for 6 to 12 hours, stirring occasionally.

At serving-time, place the chicken pieces, skin side up, on a large broiling rack. Do not overlap them. Reserve the marinade. Cook the chicken in a preheated broiler, 4 inches from the flame, for 15 minutes. Then, turn the pieces, baste them with the reserved marinade, and broil 10 minutes longer. Serve immediately.

Serves 3 to 4.

Accompanying dishes:
Craftsman: artichokes, breaded cauliflower, noodles, green salad
Editors: Herbed Rice*, Steamed "Kamada" Squash*

CHICKEN CUTLET ALLA GRIPPI

JAMIE BENNETT

- 3 large chicken breasts, skinned, boned and halved
- 3 eggs, beaten
- 1 cup bread crumbs
- 2 tablespoons finely chopped parsley
- 1 teaspoon oregano
- 1 tablespoon dried basil
- ¼ cup grated Parmesan cheese
- ¼ cup salad oil
- 1 clove garlic, peeled

Place the six chicken breast halves in the beaten eggs and set aside for at least 1 hour.

At serving-time, combine the bread crumbs, parsley, oregano, basil and Parmesan cheese. Spread the mixture out in a large shallow bowl or platter. In a 12-inch skillet, heat the salad oil with the garlic clove and when the garlic is brown, discard it. Remove one chicken breast-half at a time from the egg mixture and gently roll it in the seasoned crumbs to coat it evenly. Place it in the hot oil and repeat the procedure until all the chicken is coated and cooking. Fry for 4 to 6 minutes on each side, then serve immediately.

Serves 4 to 6.

Accompanying dishes:
Craftsman: artichokes or broccoli, green salad
Editors: Herbed Rice* or wild rice, salad

CHINESE CHICKEN AND TOMATOES

WILHELMINA GODFREY

2 tablespoons soy sauce
1 teaspoon sugar
2 tablespoons dry sherry
1 tablespoon cornstarch, plus ¼ cup cornstarch
1½ pounds boned chicken breast, cut in 1-inch pieces
1 large onion, peeled and cut in 8 wedges
2 large tomatoes, peeled and cut in 1-inch dice
½ cup salad oil
½ cup chicken stock

This Chinese dish uses the "stir-fry" technique; thus it is essential that everything be prepared ahead of time, ready for instant cooking action:
1. In a small bowl combine one tablespoon of the soy sauce with the sugar and 1 tablespoon of the dry sherry. Add the tablespoon of cornstarch and mix until they are well blended. Set aside until ready to use.
2. In a shallow bowl combine the remaining tablespoons of soy sauce and sherry. On a paper towel, next to the chicken, sprinkle the remaining ¼ cup of cornstarch.
3. Place the chicken pieces, onion wedges and diced tomatoes within easy reach on separate plates.

About 10 minutes before you plan to serve this dish, heat the oil in a 12- to 14-inch skillet or large wok. Meanwhile drop the chicken pieces in the shallow bowl of soy sauce and sherry (step 2), turning them so that all sides are thoroughly moistened. Shake off the excess liquid and gently roll the pieces in the cornstarch until they are lightly coated. When the oil is at the smoking point, drop the chicken into the skillet or wok and cook over high heat about 2 minutes, stirring constantly. Add the onion wedges and, stirring constantly, cook them until they just become translucent, about 2 minutes longer. With a slotted spoon, immediately transfer the chicken and onions to a serving platter and reserve.

Drain off all but 1 tablespoon of the oil from the skillet or wok. Lower the heat to medium and add the contents of the small bowl (step 1)—the soy sauce, sherry and sugar. Stir for a few minutes until the sauce has absorbed the oil and has thickened somewhat. Pour in the chicken stock and bring to a boil, stirring constantly to prevent lumps from forming. Return the chicken and onions to the skillet and drop in the tomato dice. Mix well and stir-fry until heated—no longer than 5 minutes.

Serves 4.

Accompanying dishes:
Craftsman: rice, green vegetable and Chinese tea

BAKED CHICKEN WITH BROWN RICE

KAREN KARNES

2 cups chicken stock
1 teaspoon salt
¼ teaspoon freshly ground black pepper
1 cup brown rice
1 pound carrots, scraped and cut into 1-inch slices
2 medium-sized onions, peeled and cut into eight pieces
2 tablespoons finely chopped parsley
   A 3-pound chicken, cut into eight pieces
½ pound fresh peas (optional)

In a large, flame-proof casserole that is at least 12 inches in diameter, bring the chicken stock to a boil. Drop in the salt, pepper and rice and stir well. Mix in the carrots, onions and parsley, then carefully place the chicken pieces, skin side up, on the vegetables. Do not overlap them. Cover the casserole and bake in a preheated 375° oven for 1 hour. If you are using the peas, remove the casserole from the oven after 45 minutes. Lift out the chicken and scatter the peas over the rice-and-carrot mixture. Return the chicken to the casserole, skin side up, and bake covered 15 minutes longer. Serve immediately.

Serves 3 to 4.

Accompanying dishes:
*Editors: Spinach and Orange Salad**

BAKED CHICKEN WITH SHERRY AND GRAPES

PHILLIP WARD

4 whole chicken breasts
1 clove garlic, peeled and cut in half
⅔ cup cream sherry
1 teaspoon dried thyme
½ teaspoon dried marjoram
1 teaspoon salt
½ teaspoon freshly ground black pepper
2 cups seedless grapes

Rub the chicken breasts with the cut surfaces of the garlic, then discard the garlic. Place the chicken in a large baking pan and pour the sherry over it. Turn the pieces once or twice to coat them evenly with the sherry, then sprinkle with the thyme, marjoram, salt and pepper. Scatter the grapes among the chicken pieces. Cover the pan tightly with heavy duty aluminum foil and bake in a preheated 425° oven for 30 minutes.

Remove the foil, baste the chicken with the pan juices and return them, uncovered, to the oven. Brown them 15 minutes. Serve immediately.

Serves 4.

Accompanying dishes:
Craftsman: rice, string beans with slivered almonds or broccoli with brown butter
Editors: Bulgur with Broccoli and Tomatoes*, tossed green salad

GARLIC-LEMON CHICKEN

ZELDA STRECKER

2 tablespoons butter
2 tablespoons oil
One 3-pound frying chicken, cut into 8 pieces
2 teaspoons finely chopped garlic
¼ cup finely chopped onions
1 teaspoon dried marjoram
1 teaspoon salt
¼ teaspoon freshly ground black pepper
¼ cup dry white wine
1 lemon, sliced very thin

In a 12- to 14-inch skillet, heat the butter and oil to the smoking point. Drop in the chicken pieces and fry them over high heat until they are brown on both sides. Immediately reduce the heat. Transfer the chicken pieces to a heated platter and set it aside. In the same skillet sauté the garlic and onions over low heat until they are soft and translucent.

Return the chicken to the skillet, turning the pieces once or twice to coat them with the garlic and onions. Season it with the marjoram, salt and pepper, then pour in the wine. Arrange the lemon slices on the chicken, then cover the skillet and cook over low heat 15 minutes longer. Serve immediately.

Serves 4.

Accompanying dishes:
Craftsman: Salad, herbed-and-buttered French bread
*Editors: Bulgur with Broccoli and Tomatoes**

MADAME RENOIR'S CHICKEN
MARILYN PAPPAS

¼ cup olive oil
   A 3- to 3½-pound chicken, cut into eight pieces
2 tablespoons butter
1 teaspoon finely chopped garlic
½ cup finely chopped onions
2 tomatoes, peeled and chopped
2 sprigs parsley
½ teaspoon dried thyme, or 1 teaspoon finely minced fresh thyme
1 teaspoon salt
½ teaspoon freshly ground black pepper
¾ cup dry white wine
12 small mushroom caps, stems discarded
12 black olives, pitted
¼ cup cognac
¼ cup finely chopped parsley

In a heavy 12- to 14-inch skillet, heat the oil to the smoking point. Add the chicken pieces and sauté them over high heat until they are browned on both sides. Remove them with tongs or a slotted spoon to a flameproof casserole. Drain and discard any oil remaining in the skillet.

In the same skillet, melt the butter and when it foams, sauté the garlic and onions over low to medium heat for several minutes, until they are soft and somewhat translucent. Then add the chopped tomatoes, parsley, thyme, salt and pepper and cook 2 to 3 minutes longer, or until the tomatoes release their liquid. Stir as you cook, scraping up any chicken bits that might have adhered to the bottom of the skillet. Add the white wine, bring it to a boil, then pour the contents of the skillet over the chicken.

Cook the chicken, covered, over low heat for 15 minutes. Then drop in the mushroom caps and pitted olives and simmer 15 minutes longer. Just before serving, heat the cognac in a small saucepan, ignite it, and when the flame dies down, pour it over the chicken. Sprinkle with the parsley and serve.

Serves 4.

Accompanying dishes:
Editors: baby new potatoes in their skins, green salad

CHICKEN BURIYANI

MEL SOMEROSKI

¼ cup salad oil
    A 3-pound chicken cut into eight pieces
⅛ teaspoon cinnamon
⅛ teaspoon ground nutmeg
⅛ teaspoon cayenne
1 teaspoon celery flakes
2 tablespoons finely chopped parsley
⅛ teaspoon turmeric
⅛ teaspoon ground cloves
⅛ teaspoon ground ginger
1 tablespoon garam masala,
    or 1 tablespoon curry powder
⅛ teaspoon freshly ground black pepper
⅛ teaspoon ground cardamom
⅛ teaspoon paprika
1 tablespoon salt
1 tablespoon finely chopped green chili pepper
¼ cup tomato paste
3¼ cups chicken stock or water
3 medium-sized onions, thinly sliced
¼ cup coarsely chopped walnuts
¼ cup seedless raisins
1 cup brown rice

In a 12- to 14-inch skillet heat the salad oil to the smoking point over a high flame. Fry the chicken pieces until they are golden brown on all sides, then remove them with a slotted spoon or tongs to a flame-proof casserole. This takes about 10 minutes.

While the chicken is frying, prepare the spices: place all the herbs and spices in a small bowl along with the salt and chili pepper. Add the tomato paste and ¾ cup of the chicken stock or water and blend until smooth.

When all the chicken is done, lower the heat, and sauté the onions in the fat remaining in the skillet until they are soft. With the slotted spoon or tongs transfer the onions to paper towels to drain before adding them to the chicken pieces in the casserole. Pour off all the oil remaining in the skillet and cook the spice mixture for 2 to 3 minutes to allow the flavors to develop. Add the walnuts and raisins to the casserole, then pour the slightly thickened warm spice mixture over the contents of the casserole. Stir in the remaining 2½ cups of chicken stock or water and, finally, add the brown rice, stirring well so that all the grains are covered by the liquid. Bring to a boil, then lower the heat and cover the casserole. Simmer 1 hour. Remove the lid and cook 15 minutes longer so that the rice dries somewhat and the sauce thickens. Serve immediately, or reheat when you are ready to serve.

Serves 4.

Accompanying dishes:
Editors: Raita*
Craftsman: chutney, yoghurt, Tomato Sambal*, eggplant curry, shredded coconut, mixed nuts, sliced bananas

CHICKEN AND WILD RICE CASSEROLE

WARREN MACKENZIE

1 cup wild rice
2 teaspoons salt
6 tablespoons butter
1 teaspoon finely chopped garlic
2 cups coarsely chopped onions
½ pound mushrooms, thinly sliced
2 cups finely chopped celery
1 cup scraped and thinly sliced carrots
1 teaspoon dried basil
1 teaspoon dried tarragon
½ teaspoon freshly ground black pepper
½ cup dry white wine
½ cup chicken stock
3 to 4 cups cooked, diced chicken

Rinse the wild rice well. Bring 6 to 8 cups of water to a boil, add 1 teaspoon of the salt and the rice. Stir to make sure none of the rice sticks to the bottom of the pan, then, when the water resumes its boil, lower the heat and simmer, uncovered, for 45 minutes or until the rice is tender. Drain and set aside.

Meanwhile, in a 12- to 14-inch skillet, heat the butter until it foams. Add the garlic and onions and sauté until they are soft, about 5 minutes. Drop the mushrooms into the skillet, and cook until their liquid has evaporated. Then stir in the celery and carrots, the herbs, the remaining teaspoon of salt, the pepper, white wine and chicken stock and cook for 5 minutes until the celery and carrots are barely tender.

In a large oven-proof casserole, combine the vegetables, the wild rice and the chicken dice. Taste for seasoning and add more salt if necessary. Thirty minutes before serving, cover the casserole and bake in a preheated 300° oven for 30 minutes. Serve immediately.

Serves 6 to 8.

Accompanying dishes:
Craftsman: green salad
Editors: Spinach Salad or Tabbouleh**

CHICKEN PILAF WITH EGGPLANT

PHYLLIS YACOPINO

1 medium-sized eggplant,
   peeled and cut into ½-inch slices
2 teaspoons salt
1 pound Italian sausage, either "hot" or "sweet" or a
   combination of the two, skins removed
1¼ cups olive oil
1 cup coarsely chopped onions
2 cups seeded and coarsely chopped green peppers
2 large tomatoes, peeled and chopped,
2 large tomatoes, peeled and chopped, plus 2 large
   tomatoes, peeled and cut into ½-inch slices
1½ cups brown rice
¼ teaspoon dried thyme
¼ cup finely chopped parsley
½ teaspoon white pepper
2 cups chicken stock
3 cups cooked chicken, cut into bite-sized pieces
½ cup pimiento-stuffed olives, sliced, plus ½ cup

whole pimiento-stuffed olives
½ cup grated Parmesan cheese

Place the eggplant slices in a colander, sprinkle them with 1 teaspoon of the salt and weight them down with a heavy object such as a cast-iron skillet. Set them aside to drain at least ½ hour.

Meanwhile, in a 10- to 12-inch skillet, fry the sausage until it has lost its red, raw appearance. Remove it with a slotted spoon to a plate and drain on paper towels to absorb the excess oil.

Pour ¼ cup of the olive oil into a large flame-proof casserole and sauté the onions and peppers until they are soft and the onions are translucent. Add the chopped tomatoes and cook until their liquid has evaporated. Pour in the brown rice, stirring well to coat each grain with liquid. Then mix in the sausage meat, the thyme, parsley, pepper and the remaining teaspoon of salt. Pour in the chicken stock, cover and bring the liquid to a boil. Reduce the heat and simmer for 35 minutes, or until the rice is just tender. If the rice is not dry at this point, remove the cover and cook 5 minutes longer.

While the rice is cooking, pour ½ cup of the remaining olive oil into a skillet and, over medium heat, bring it to the smoking point. Fry the eggplant slices until they are brown on both sides, using the last ½ cup of olive oil if necessary. As they cook, remove the slices to paper towels to drain.

Stir the chicken pieces and sliced olives into the sausage-and-rice mixture. Then, alternately place tomato and eggplant slices over the rice, around the edge of the casserole. Arrange the whole olives decoratively in the center and sprinkle with the grated Parmesan cheese. Broil 6 inches from the flame for 5 minutes, or until the cheese melts and its surface is lightly browned.

Serves 8.

Accompanying dishes:
Craftsman: antipasto, garlic bread
*Editors: a green vegetable, such as broccoli or Polish Zucchini**

WYMAN'S CHICKEN CASSEROLE

WILLIAM WYMAN

3 tablespoons butter
3 tablespoons salad oil
1 teaspoon salt
¼ teaspoon freshly ground black pepper
   A 3-pound frying chicken, cut into 8 pieces
1½ cups coarsely chopped onion
1 teaspoon finely chopped garlic
1 green pepper, seeded and sliced
1 cup chopped celery
1 teaspoon dried tarragon
1 tablespoon chopped parsley
½ cup dry white wine

In a 12-inch skillet, heat the butter and salad oil until they are very hot. Rub the salt and pepper into the chicken skin, then sauté the pieces over high heat until both sides are golden brown. With a slotted spoon or tongs, remove them to an oven-proof casserole.

In the oil remaining in the skillet and over low heat, sauté the onion, garlic, green pepper and celery until they are soft, about 5 minutes. Sprinkle in the tarragon and parsley and cook 1 or 2 minutes longer. Carefully transfer the vegetables to the casserole, draining off as much of the oil as possible. Stir the contents of the casserole to distribute the vegetables evenly. Then pour in the wine, cover and bring the liquid to a boil. Transfer the casserole to a preheated 350° oven and bake for 30 minutes.

Serves 4.

Accompanying dishes:
Craftsman: rice or noodles, salad, French bread
Editors: Baked Rice*, salad

QUICK COUS-COUS

CAROLE LYNNE LUBOVE

3 tablespoons butter
2 tablespoons salad oil
   A 3-pound frying chicken, cut into 8 pieces
2 teaspoons finely chopped garlic
½ cup coarsely chopped onions
2 medium-sized carrots, scraped and sliced
½ teaspoon allspice
1 teaspoon turmeric
1 teaspoon ground cumin
   One 20-ounce can chick peas, drained
4 cups chicken stock

2 teaspoons salt
¼ teaspoon freshly ground black pepper
1½ cups cous-cous

In a large flame-proof casserole, heat the butter and oil until the butter foams. Add the chicken pieces and sauté over medium to high heat until the chicken is browned on all sides. With tongs, or a slotted spoon, transfer the chicken to a platter and reserve.

In the oil remaining in the casserole, sauté the garlic and onions over low heat until they are limp. Add the carrots, allspice, turmeric, and cumin and, stirring frequently, cook for 5 minutes. Then add the chick peas, chicken stock, salt and pepper. Cover, and bring the liquid to a boil. Return the chicken pieces to the casserole, lower the heat, cover and simmer 15 minutes. Turn off the heat. Pour in the cous-cous, mix well and cover. Allow the mixture to rest 15 minutes, while the cous-cous absorbs the liquid in the casserole. Then serve immediately.

Serves 6.

Accompanying dishes:
Editors: watercress and endive salad

BOUILLABAISSE

WILHELMINA GODFREY

½ cup olive oil
2 teaspoons finely chopped garlic
2 cups finely chopped onions
½ cup scraped and finely chopped carrots
4 large tomatoes, peeled and chopped
1 bay leaf
½ teaspoon saffron
1 teaspoon fennel (optional)
1 teaspoon salt
¼ teaspoon freshly ground black pepper
¼ cup finely chopped parsley,
    plus 1 tablespoon finely chopped parsley
1 cup dry white wine
1 cup water
2 pounds fresh fish fillets, cut into 2-inch pieces
    (striped bass, haddock, blue, etc.)
    A 3- to 4-pound lobster, cut into 2-inch pieces
12 cherrystone clams
½ pound shrimp

In a very large flame-proof casserole, heat the oil over low to medium heat. Add the garlic, onions and carrots, and sauté, stirring occasionally, for about 8 minutes until they are soft. Add the chopped tomatoes and cook 5 to 8 minutes longer, until they have released their liquid. Stir in the bay leaf, saffron, fennel, if you are using it, the salt, pepper, ¼ cup of the chopped parsley, the wine and water.

Arrange the fish pieces over the tomato mixture, cover them with the lobster pieces and, finally, add the clams. Cover the casserole and bake it in a preheated 375° oven for 40 minutes. Then, add the shrimp, cover again, and bake 5 minutes longer, or until the shrimp are pink.

Serve in large soup bowls with generous quantities of broth, and garnished with the remaining tablespoon of parsley.

Serves 6.

Accompanying dishes:
Craftsman: salad and French bread
Editors: broccoli with oil and lemon juice, French bread

SHRIMP MULLIGAN

MIKE NEVELSON

3 tablespoons salad oil
3 teaspoons finely chopped garlic
4 medium-sized onions, peeled, quartered and separated
6 large celery stalks, cut into ¼-inch slices
4 large green peppers, seeded and cut into ¼-inch slices
  Three 1-pound cans tomatoes, including their liquid
1 tablespoon cornstarch
2 tablespoons dry sherry
½ teaspoon Tabasco
1 tablespoon salt
½ teaspoon freshly ground black pepper
1 teaspoon celery seed
  Two 10-ounce packages frozen sliced okra
3 cups fresh bean sprouts* or
    two 1-pound cans bean sprouts, drained
2 pounds shrimp, peeled and deveined

Pour the salad oil into a 6- to 8-quart flame-proof casserole, and toss in the garlic and onion pieces. Cover, and steam over low to medium heat, stirring occasionally, for 15 minutes, or until the onions are limp. Add the celery and green peppers, stir to mix the vegetables, cover, and cook 10 minutes longer. Pour in the tomatoes and their liquid, bring it to a boil, cover and simmer for 15 minutes.

Meanwhile, in a small bowl, combine the cornstarch, sherry and the Tabasco and stir them to make a smooth paste. Add them to the vegetables with the salt, pepper and celery seed. Blend well. Drop in the okra, cover, and cook for 8 minutes. Finally, add the bean sprouts and the shrimp, stir two or three times, and cook, covered, 5 minutes longer. Serve immediately in deep soup bowls, on a bed of steaming rice.

Serves 8 to 10.

Accompanying dishes:
Editors: rice and salad.

*See index

SHRIMP WITH MUSHROOMS
JOHN JESSIMAN

¼ cup butter, plus 2 tablespoons butter
½ cup thinly sliced scallions, including 2 inches
    of green tops
½ pound mushrooms, thinly sliced
2 pounds fresh shrimp, peeled and deveined
3 tablespoons flour
1¼ cups light cream
¼ cup dry sherry
1 teaspoon salt
½ teaspoon white pepper
2 tablespoons finely chopped parsley

In a 12-inch skillet, melt ¼ cup of the butter over medium heat. When it foams, toss in the scallions and cook, stirring occasionally, until they are soft. Add the sliced mushrooms, and after they release their juices and there is a fair amount of liquid in the pan, stir in the shrimp. Continue to stir, until the shrimp just turn pink, about 3 to 4 minutes. Remove the skillet from the heat and set aside.

In a medium-sized saucepan, melt the remaining 2 tablespoons of butter. Add the flour and stir for 1 or 2 minutes to cook the flour somewhat and eliminate its raw taste. Very gradually, and over low heat, pour in the cream, stirring constantly to keep the sauce smooth. Add the sherry, salt and pepper. Cook until the sauce is thick and nearly at a boil. Pour it over the shrimp and mushroom mixture. Stir well to coat the shrimp evenly and serve immediately or reheat at serving-time. (Reheat over low heat and only for a short time—until the sauce and shrimp are heated through.) Garnish with the parsley.

Serves 4.

Accompanying dishes:
Editors: Toast points or Herbed Rice*, green vegetable or salad

SHRIMP AND CHINESE SNOW PEAS

JENNIFER LEW

1 teaspoon finely chopped garlic
2 pounds large shrimp, shelled and deveined
1 cup thinly sliced celery (cut diagonally)
1 large onion, halved and cut into small wedges
½ pound mushrooms, thinly sliced
½ cup thinly sliced water chestnuts
¼ pound fresh Chinese snow peas, or
    1 package frozen snow peas, partially thawed
2 tablespoons dry sherry
1 teaspoon sugar
1 tablespoon soy sauce
1 tablespoon cornstarch mixed with 2 tablespoons water
2 teaspoons salt
3 tablespoons salad oil

This dish is based on the Chinese stir-fry cooking technique. It is very important that all the ingredients be prepared ahead of time and be at the cook's fingertips for instant action!

Place the garlic on a small plate. Wash the shrimp and set them on a second plate. On a third plate, arrange the celery, onions, mushrooms and water chestnuts, then place the snow peas on a fourth plate.

In a small bowl, combine and mix the sherry, sugar, soy sauce and the cornstarch-and-water mixture. Add the salt and stir until it has dissolved.

When you are ready to serve, follow these steps:

1. In a heavy cast-iron skillet, heat the oil to the smoking point. Drop in the garlic, stir once or twice, then add the shrimp. Cook over medium heat, stirring constantly, for 1 minute, or until the shrimp just turn pink.

2. Add the celery, onions, mushrooms and water chestnuts. Stir, then add the snow peas. Mix well, cover the skillet and cook 2 to 3 minutes.

3. Remove the lid and pour in the soy sauce mixture. Stir until the sauce barely thickens, about 1 minute, and serve immediately.

Serves 4.

Accompanying dishes:
Craftsman: white rice
*Editors: rice and Sunomono**

TEMPURA (FRIED SHELLFISH AND VEGETABLES)

TOSHIKO TAKAEZU

Batter:
- 3 cups warm water
- 3 tablespoons salt
- ½ teaspoon monosodium glutamate
- 2½ cups flour
- 4 eggs

Dipping Sauce:
- 2 ounces Chinese or Japanese dried mushrooms
- 4 cups water
- 1 tablespoon sugar
- ½ cup soy sauce
- ¼ teaspoon peeled and finely chopped ginger root, plus 10 thin slices peeled ginger root
- 1 teaspoon monosodium glutamate
- 2 large shrimp
- ½ cup sake or dry white wine
- 10 lime peel twists

Shellfish and Vegetables:
- 1 pound jumbo shrimp, peeled but with tail shell intact
- ½ pound large shrimp, peeled but with tail shell intact
- ½ pound bay scallops, washed and patted dry with paper towels
- Salt

2 medium-sized onions,
   peeled and cut into ¼-inch slices
½ pound green beans, washed and the ends removed
1 large green pepper, seeded and cut into ½-inch strips
½ pound mushrooms, cut into ¼-inch slices
2 cups parsley sprigs, washed and tough ends removed
One 1-pound eggplant, cut into ¼-inch slices and
   soaked for 30 minutes in salted water to cover
1 large sweet potato, peeled and cut into ¼-inch slices
One 2-ounce package cellophane noodles,
   cut into 4-inch strands
Salad oil

To make the batter: In a medium-sized bowl, combine the warm water, salt and monosodium glutamate and stir until the dry ingredients are dissolved. Add the flour and beat until the mixture is smooth. Add the eggs, one at at time, beating well after each addition. Set aside.

To make the dipping sauce: In a 2- to 3-quart saucepan, cover the dried mushrooms with the 4 cups of water. Bring the water to a boil, reduce the heat and simmer, uncovered, over very low heat for 30 minutes. Add the sugar, soy sauce, chopped ginger, monosodium glutamate, and the 2 shrimp. Stir once or twice and continue to simmer for 15 minutes. Finally, add the sake or white wine and cook 5 minutes longer. Strain, discarding the mushrooms and the ginger and shrimp. Serve in individual bowls each garnished with a twist of lime and a slice of ginger.

When you are ready to prepare the tempura—and it must be eaten very hot, just as it comes out of the pan—pour 3 inches of the salad oil into a deep fryer or skillet. Heat the oil until it smokes or registers 400° on a deep-fat thermometer.

Prepare all the ingredients in advance and have them close at hand. The jumbo and large shrimp should be almost completely split in half lengthwise, spread flat so they are butterflied, washed, intestinal veins removed, and placed in separate mounds on paper towels. Pat them dry with paper towels. Set the scallops on another paper towel and sprinkle both scallops and shrimp with salt. Line a platter with paper towels and place it near the deep fryer. Have a slotted spoon at hand.

When the oil is hot, cook the ingredients in the following order:
1. jumbo shrimp
2. scallops
3. onion slices
4. green beans
5. green pepper slices
6. mushrooms
7. parsley sprigs
8. eggplant slices
9. sweet potato slices
10. large shrimp with cellophane noodles

Dip the jumbo shrimp into the batter, coating all but the tail. Gently slide them into the oil and fry until they are brown on both sides. Transfer to paper towels to drain. Serve the jumbo shrimp while you cook the next ingredient, using the same technique. To cook the large shrimp and cellophane noodles, place a few noodles in your left hand. Top them with a large shrimp and cover with more noodles. Holding the package so that it does not separate, dip the entire package into the batter. As the batter fries it will harden around the package, binding the ingredients. Fry as above.

As the cook, you will be busy while the guests eat, so reserve one item from each of the ingredients to make yourself an assortment of tempura just before you join the guests.

Eat the tempura with your fingers, or with chopsticks, dipping each ingredient into the sauce.

Serves 10.

Editors' comments: *You can also serve tempura by presenting all the raw ingredients at the table and inviting each guest to cook his own from a fryer placed in the center of the table.*

Accompanying dishes:
*Craftsman: Sunomono**

'INDIAN' FRIED FISH

CYNTHIA SCHIRA

¼ cup butter
¾ cup coarsely chopped onions
1 teaspoon turmeric or curry powder
½ teaspoon grated fresh ginger, or ¼ teaspoon ground ginger
1 pound fish fillets—haddock, flounder, striped bass, scrod
¼ teaspoon salt
Pinch freshly ground black pepper

In a 10- to 12-inch skillet, melt the butter over moderate heat. When it foams, drop in the onions and sauté them, stirring frequently, until they are soft. Then sprinkle in the turmeric and ginger, lower the heat and stir 1 to 2 minutes longer to develop the flavors. Add the fish fillets, spoon the onion-and-spice mixture over them, cover and cook for 4 to 7 minutes on each side. Just before serving, season with the salt and pepper. Serve immediately.

Serves 2.

Accompanying dishes:
Craftsman: Raita*, rice or potatoes, green vegetable

BARBECUED FISH STEAKS

DON REITZ

1 tablespoon sugar
¼ teaspoon salt
¼ cup wine vinegar
¼ cup dry sherry
2 tablespoons soy sauce
1 teaspoon peeled and finely grated ginger root
½ teaspoon finely chopped garlic
⅛ teaspoon freshly ground black pepper
½ cup olive oil
6 fresh fish steaks, about 1½ inches thick (striped bass, halibut, swordfish)

Make a marinade by combining the sugar, salt, vinegar, sherry and soy sauce in a 9-by-13-by-2-inch baking dish. Stir until the sugar and salt are dissolved. Then, add the grated ginger, garlic, pepper and olive oil. Blend thoroughly. Gently set the fish steaks in the marinade and turn them to coat both sides. Marinate at room temperature for at least 3 hours, turning them once or twice. Or, if you prefer, the steaks may be marinated in the refrigerator, in which case you should allow 5 to 6 hours for the process. Return them to room temperature before cooking.

Allow 45 minutes to prepare the charcoal fire—the coals should be red, without any evidence of flame. Make certain the surface of the grill is well oiled. Set the grill 3 inches above the charcoal. Place the fish steaks on it, baste them generously with the marinade and broil for 5 minutes, then turn the fish steaks. Baste again and broil 5 minutes longer. Repeat this procedure twice or until the fish has cooked for 20 minutes. Serve immediately.

Serves 6.

Editors' comments: *The steaks may also be cooked about 3 inches from a broiler flame, following the same technique.*

BAKED HADDOCK WITH LEMON SAUCE

PRISCILLA MERRITT

1 teaspoon butter, softened, plus 2 tablespoons butter
2 pounds haddock fillets
½ teaspoon salt
¼ teaspoon white pepper
1 tablespoon onion juice
8 medium-sized mushrooms

Sauce:
2 tablespoons butter
2 tablespoons flour
½ cup lemon juice
½ cup fish stock, white wine or water
½ teaspoon salt
1 teaspoon sugar
2 tablespoons finely chopped parsley

Grease an oven-proof baking pan with the teaspoon of softened butter. In it, arrange the haddock fillets, skin side down. Sprinkle them with salt, pepper and onion juice. Dot the fillets with the remaining 2 tablespoons of butter. Separate the mushroom stems from their caps; slice the stems but leave the caps whole. Scatter the stems over the fish and arrange the caps decoratively on the fillets. Cover the pan tightly with aluminum foil, and bake in a preheated 350° oven for 30 to 40 minutes, or until the fish flakes easily and is opaque.

Meanwhile, make the sauce: melt the 2 tablespoons of butter in a small saucepan and add the flour. Stir briskly over low heat for a few minutes to cook the flour somewhat and eliminate its raw taste. Then, slowly pour in the lemon juice, stock or wine or water, beating constantly to keep the sauce smooth. Add the salt and sugar. Cook the sauce, stirring it constantly, until it is thick. Finally, sprinkle in the parsley.

When you are ready to serve the fish, warm the sauce to the simmering point. Then, with a spatula, transfer the fillets to a hot platter. Pour the juices from the baking pan into the sauce and stir to blend well. Pour the sauce over the fish and serve immediately.

Serves 4.

Accompanying dishes:
Craftsman: sweet potatoes, green vegetable
*Editors: boiled potatoes with parsley, Garden Vegetable Casserole**

STEAMED STUFFED TROUT
HARVEY LITTLETON

Stuffing:
 1 medium-sized green pepper, seeded and julienned
 1 medium-sized onion, peeled and very thinly sliced
 ¾ cup scraped and very thinly sliced carrots
 2 large tomatoes, cut into ¼-inch slices
 ½ cup finely chopped parsley
 1 tablespoon finely chopped fresh sage
 1 teaspoon finely chopped fresh tarragon
 1 teaspoon salt
 ¼ teaspoon freshly ground black pepper

 One 5-pound trout, cleaned, back and rib bones
  removed, head and tail intact
 1 medium-sized onion, peeled and thinly sliced
 1 medium-sized green pepper, seeded and julienned
 1 teaspoon salt
 ½ teaspoon freshly ground black pepper
 ¼ cup dry sherry
 ¼ cup finely chopped parsley

To make the stuffing: Combine the pepper, onion, carrots, tomatoes, parsley, sage, tarragon, salt and pepper and toss to mix the ingredients thoroughly.

Packing it loosely, stuff the mixture into the trout's cavity. With a needle and strong thread, sew up the cavity.

98

Along the center of a sheet of heavy duty aluminum foil at least 10 inches longer than the trout, scatter ½ the remaining onion and green pepper slices and sprinkle them with ½ teaspoon of the salt and ¼ teaspoon of the pepper. Place the stuffed trout on the mixture, and arrange the remaining onions, peppers, salt and pepper on top. Fold the foil over the trout's head and tail. Then, bring the two side sections of foil together and fold them over each other several times so as to make as airtight a package as possible. Before completely sealing the package pour in the sherry.

Bake the trout in a preheated 425° oven for 1¼ hours. Remove it from the foil package and arrange it on a heated platter, garnishing it with the remaining ¼ cup of parsley. Serve immediately.

Serves 4 to 6.

QUICHE LORRAINE

AILEEN O. WEBB

One 9-inch unbaked pie shell
1½ cups light cream
1 cup coarsely grated Swiss cheese
4 eggs, well beaten
½ teaspoon salt
¼ teaspoon white pepper
Pinch of cayenne
½ cup cooked and drained bacon, crumbled, or substitute ham, chicken or turkey cut into ½-inch dice

Line the unbaked pie shell with aluminum foil. To weight the pastry, mound some rice, dried beans or peas in the center. This will keep the shell from shrinking as it bakes. Bake it in a preheated 425° oven for 10 minutes, remove the weight and foil, lower the oven temperature to 350°, and bake the shell 15 minutes longer. Remove from the oven and cool.

To make the filling: In a medium-sized saucepan, bring the cream to a slow simmer, then gradually add the grated cheese, stirring constantly so that it melts. Do not let the cream boil. When all the cheese has been added, very slowly pour the contents of the saucepan into the eggs, beating constantly. Sprinkle in the salt, white pepper and cayenne.

Pour the filling into the baked pie shell. Evenly distribute the bacon, ham, chicken or turkey pieces on the filling; they will sink beneath the surface. Bake the pie in a preheated 325° oven for 40 minutes, or until a knife inserted in its center comes out clean.

The pie may be served hot or at room temperature.

Serves 6 as a luncheon course
8 to 10 as an hors d'oeuvre

Accompanying dishes:
Editors: lettuce and tomato salad or Spinach Salad*, if you are serving the Quiche Lorraine at lunch.

OMELET WITH YOGHURT AND ALFALFA SPROUTS

PAUL SOLDNER

2 eggs
2 teaspoons dry white wine
½ teaspoon finely minced fresh dill weed
¼ teaspoon dried marjoram
¼ teaspoon salt
   Freshly ground black pepper
1 tablespoon butter
½ teaspoon salad oil
1 tablespoon yoghurt
1 tablespoon alfalfa sprouts, or 1 tablespoon chopped
   bean sprouts*

In a bowl, combine the eggs, wine, dill weed, marjoram, salt and pepper and beat vigorously 30 seconds.

In an 8- to 10-inch heavy skillet, heat the butter and oil until the butter foams, then pour in the beaten egg mixture. Cook the omelet over medium heat, tipping the eggs in the pan and gently lifting the cooked portion to allow the uncooked mixture to run under it.

In a small bowl, combine the yoghurt and alfalfa sprouts and mix them well. When the omelet is nearly done, but its surface is still liquid, spread the yoghurt-and-alfalfa mixture over half of its surface. Turn off the heat, then fold the omelet over onto itself.

Serve immediately.

Serves 1.

*See index

LUNCHEON MUSHROOMS

PAT SCARLETT

3 tablespoons butter
½ pound mushrooms, cut into ¼-inch slices
2 tablespoons finely minced fresh basil, or
   ½ teaspoon dried basil
½ teaspoon salt
   Freshly ground black pepper
2 tablespoons dry white wine
½ cup sour cream
½ cup finely grated Swiss cheese (optional)

In a 10-inch skillet, melt the butter and when it foams, lower the heat and sauté the mushrooms with the basil sprinkled over them, until the mushrooms are delicately browned. Do not allow them to cook to the point where they release their juices. Sprinkle with the salt and pepper, add the white wine and sour cream, and mixing quickly, cook only until the cream is thoroughly distributed.

Serve immediately over toast points or toasted English muffins, with the Swiss cheese sprinkled on top, if you are using it.

Serves 2.

Accompanying dishes:
Editors: Tomato and lettuce salad

HAM IN JELLIED HERB SAUCE

DENA TODD

One 10½-ounce can chicken stock
1 package unflavored gelatine
¼ cup mayonnaise
1 teaspoon dried tarragon
1 teaspoon Dijon-type mustard
¼ teaspoon mixed salad herbs
1 teaspoon lime marmalade
½ cup finely chopped fresh parsley, plus 1 tablespoon
   finely chopped fresh parsley
1 teaspoon salad oil
   Six to eight ¼-inch slices canned ham

In a small saucepan, heat the chicken stock. Sprinkle the gelatine over the surface and stir until it is thoroughly dissolved. Cool.

Meanwhile, to make the sauce, mix the mayonnaise, tarragon, mustard, salad herbs and marmalade together.

Add ½ cup of the parsley, then pour in the cooled gelatine-and-stock and blend thoroughly.

With the salad oil, lightly grease the bottom and sides of a 7-by-9-by-2-inch baking dish. Ladle the mayonnaise sauce into the dish, then carefully arrange the ham slices in overlapping layers over the sauce. The sauce will filter through somewhat. Refrigerate until the sauce is chilled and firm.

To unmold, run a knife around the edges of the dish. Set it in a bowl of hot water for a few seconds, then remove it from the water and place the serving platter over it. Invert and shake gently until you feel the ham slip onto the platter. Garnish with the remaining tablespoon of chopped parsley.

Serves 4 to 6.

Accompanying dishes:
Craftsman: a broccoli-rice casserole, green salad
*Editors: scalloped potatoes, Garden Vegetable Casserole**

CHILE CON QUESO

CLAYTON BAILEY

2 tablespoons butter
1 teaspoon finely chopped garlic
1½ cups finely chopped onions
1 tablespoon seeded and finely chopped chili peppers
5 large tomatoes, peeled and cut into ½-inch dice
½ teaspoon salt
¼ teaspoon freshly ground black pepper
2 tablespoons flour
⅓ cup milk
½ pound coarsely grated sharp cheddar cheese

In a 12-inch skillet, melt the butter over low heat and, when it foams, add the garlic and onions. Sauté them, stirring frequently, until they are soft and translucent. Then, add the chili peppers, diced tomatoes, salt and pepper and cook the mixture until the tomatoes begin to release their liquid. Partially cover the skillet and cook 30 minutes longer, stirring occasionally.

Meanwhile, in a small bowl, combine the flour and milk and stir them to make a smooth paste. Gradually, add the grated cheese to the tomato mixture, stirring until the cheese has melted and is thoroughly blended.

Pour in the flour paste, mixing well, and cook over low heat for 1 to 2 minutes, until the chili has thickened somewhat. Serve immediately over toast points.

Serves 6.

Editors' comments: *Chile con Queso is a Mexican dish that may be served with such traditional accompaniments as refried beans, Guacamole* and tostadas. Used as a dip with corn chips, it is an unusual hors d'oeuvre.*

Accompanying dishes:
Editors: Grilled mushrooms, green salad

VEGETABLES

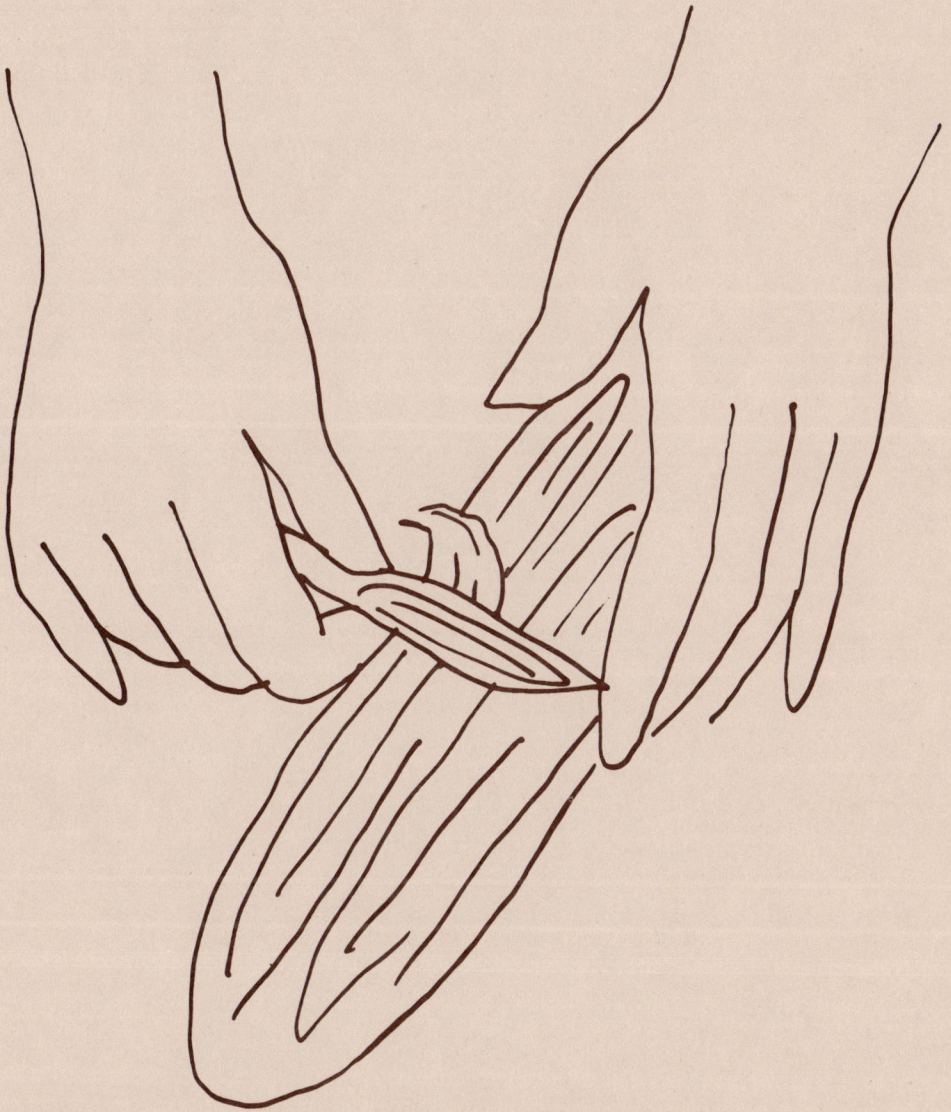

SWEET-AND-SOUR RED CABBAGE

MARY STEPHENS NELSON

¼ cup butter
½ cup finely chopped onion
½ cup light brown sugar
1 large red cabbage, coarsely sliced (about 3 pounds)
¼ cup cider vinegar
1 teaspoon salt
¼ teaspoon freshly ground black pepper
3 large apples, peeled and cut into ½-inch dice
¼ cup dry sherry

In a large flame-proof casserole, melt the butter over medium heat. When it foams, add the onions and sauté them until they are soft and translucent. Add the brown sugar and stir until it has dissolved. Then, add the cabbage, vinegar, salt, pepper and apples. Toss to mix thoroughly, and cook until the cabbage begins to steam. Cover the casserole, lower the heat, and simmer for 25 minutes. Finally, stir in the sherry and cook, covered, 5 minutes longer.

Serves 8.

APPLE SAUERKRAUT

MARY ANN SCHERR

4 tablespoons bacon drippings
1 large onion, thinly sliced
3 pounds sauerkraut, drained
3 tart apples, peeled, cored and thinly sliced
2 cups peeled and grated potatoes
2 teaspoons salt
1 teaspoon caraway seeds
½ to 1 cup dark brown sugar, according to taste
1½ cups beef stock

In a 6- to 8-quart Dutch Oven, melt the bacon drippings, then add the sliced onions and sauté them over medium heat until they are lightly browned. Add the sauerkraut, bring to a boil, cover and reduce the heat. Simmer for 5 minutes.

Add the sliced apples and grated potatoes to the contents of the Dutch Oven. Sprinkle with the salt, caraway and as much of the brown sugar as you like. With a large spoon, toss the mixture until the ingredients are thoroughly distributed. Then, pour in the stock, stir again, and bring the liquid to a boil. Reduce the heat, cover and simmer for ½ hour.

Serves 8.

BAKED CARDAMOM CARROTS

MARGRET CRAVER

1 pound carrots, scraped and cut into ¾-inch slices
1 tablespoon sugar
½ teaspoon salt
¼ teaspoon powdered cardamom
1 tablespoon water
2 tablespoons butter

In a small, oven-proof casserole equipped with a lid, combine the carrots, sugar, salt, cardamom and water. Toss to mix the ingredients. Dot the top with the butter. Cover the casserole, and bake the carrots in a preheated 325° oven for 45 minutes, or until the carrots are just tender.

Serves 3 to 4.

HONEYED CARROTS WITH CASHEWS

TED HALLMAN

1 pound carrots, scraped and cut into 1-inch slices
½ teaspoon finely chopped garlic
¼ teaspoon salt
5 teaspoons sesame oil
¼ cup coarsely chopped cashew nuts
5 teaspoons honey
2 teaspoons soy sauce
2 tablespoons sesame seeds, toasted*

In a 2- to 3-quart saucepan equipped with a lid, combine the carrots, garlic and salt and enough water to cover the bottom of the pan by about ¼ inch. Bring to a boil, cover and reduce the heat. Simmer the carrots for 15 minutes, or until they are just tender. If the carrots become dry during the cooking, add more water. When the carrots are done, drain them and transfer to a small bowl while you prepare the glaze.

Pour the sesame oil into the saucepan and heat over medium heat. Drop in the raw cashew nuts and sauté them for 1 to 3 minutes, stirring frequently until they are browned. Lower the heat and add the honey and soy sauce. Mix thoroughly, then return the carrots to the pan and stir them gently to cover them with the sauce. Cook until the carrots are heated through and shining with glaze. Sprinkle with the sesame seeds and serve hot or cold.

Serves 4.

*See index

KAJI CHON (KOREAN FRIED EGGPLANT)

ANNA KANG BURGESS

Batter:
  2 eggs
  ¾ cup water
  1 cup flour
  1 teaspoon salt, plus 1 tablespoon salt
  ¼ teaspoon freshly ground black pepper
  1 medium-sized eggplant, peeled

Dipping sauce:
  ⅓ cup soy sauce
  2 tablespoons salad oil
  2 tablespoons cider vinegar
  1 teaspoon sugar
  2 teaspoons sesame seeds, toasted*
  ¼ teaspoon freshly ground black pepper
  Oil for frying

To make the batter: In a medium-sized bowl beat the eggs and water vigorously for 1 to 2 minutes with a rotary beater. Then add the flour, 1 teaspoon of salt and the pepper and continue beating until the mixture is very smooth. Refrigerate for at least 1 hour.

Meanwhile, cut the peeled eggplant in half lengthwise and slice it crosswise into ½-inch pieces. Place the slices in a colander, sprinkle them with the tablespoon of salt and weight them down with a heavy object such as a cast-iron skillet. Set aside to drain for about 1 hour, then pat the eggplant dry with paper towels.

To make the dipping sauce: In a small bowl or bottle combine the soy sauce, salad oil, vinegar, sugar, sesame seeds and pepper and stir or shake vigorously until the sugar is dissolved. Reserve until ready to serve.

When you are ready to prepare and serve the eggplant, pour oil to a depth of ½-inch into a 12- to 14-inch skillet and heat over high flame to the smoking point. Working quickly, completely immerse each eggplant slice in the batter, then slide the pieces gently into the hot oil. Cook as many slices as you can fit into the skillet at one time, turning them after 1 to 2 minutes, when they are golden. When both sides have been cooked, transfer the slices to drain in an oven-proof dish that has been lined with paper towels. Keep the eggplant warm in a preheated 200° oven while you fry the remaining slices.

As soon as all the eggplant is prepared—and delay does not improve this dish—serve it immediately, accompanied by individual bowls of the dipping sauce.

Serves 6.

*See index

KILN-BAKED POTATOES

ELLAMARIE WOOLLEY

Baking potatoes, one per serving
Sour cream
Pecans or other nuts, coarsely chopped

Scrub the skin of the potatoes thoroughly. Pierce each potato with the point of a knife and place them unwrapped in an enameling kiln when it has cooled to 500° after firing. Bake for 40 minutes or until done.

Serve sour cream and chopped pecans in separate bowls as flavoring instead of the usual butter.

Editors' comments: *The enameling kiln at the Woolley studio measures 15" x 15". If fired to 1500° and turned off at noon, the kiln temperature reaches 500° about 4½ hours later when the potatoes are put in for an early supper.*

MIKE'S POTATOES

MICHAEL JERRY

¼ cup butter
½ cup coarsely chopped onions
3 cups peeled potatoes cut in ½-inch dice
½ teaspoon salt
¼ teaspoon white pepper
½ cup Half-and-Half
2 tablespoons finely chopped parsley

In an oven-proof casserole heat the butter until it foams and sauté the onions until they are soft. Add the diced potatoes, salt and pepper and pour in the Half-and-Half. Mix well.

Cover the casserole and place it in a preheated 325° oven to bake for 45 minutes. Remove the cover and bake 15 to 20 minutes longer, or until the top is brown. Add more Half-and-Half if the potatoes begin to dry out. Sprinkle with the parsley and serve immediately.

Serves 4.

POTATO DUMPLINGS

CYNTHIA SCHIRA

1 pound new potatoes
2½ teaspoons salt
2 eggs
1 tablespoon butter, melted
½ cup flour

Boil the potatoes in their skins until they are tender, from 15 to 30 minutes, depending on their size. Drain them and refrigerate overnight. To prepare the dumplings, peel the potatoes and force them through a ricer into a bowl. Add 1½ teaspoons of the salt, the eggs and melted butter, beating hard. Stir in the flour and blend well.

Fill a 3- to 4-quart saucepan with water and bring it to a boil, then add the remaining teaspoon of salt. Reduce the heat so the water is barely simmering and gently drop in the batter by the heaping tablespoonful. The dumplings will sink to the bottom and slowly rise to the surface as they cook. Turn them once. Cook the dumplings 15 minutes, then carefully remove them from the saucepan with a slotted spoon and serve immediately.

Yield: 10 dumplings

SWEET POTATOES WITH ORANGE-RUM GLAZE

BARBARA SHAWCROFT

1 teaspoon butter, softened, plus 6 tablespoons butter
6 medium-sized sweet potatoes, peeled
4 tablespoons honey
1 teaspoon salt
1 cup orange juice (preferably fresh orange juice)
1 teaspoon poppy seeds, crushed with a mortar
    and pestle
3 tablespoons Jamaican rum

Grease a shallow, oven-proof baking dish with the teaspoon of softened butter.

Set the sweet potatoes in a 3- to 4-quart saucepan filled with boiling salted water, lower the heat and cook the potatoes until they are tender, about 1 hour. Transfer the sweet potatoes to a rack to drain and, when they are cool enough to handle, split them in half lengthwise and arrange the halves, cut side up, in the prepared baking dish.

To make the glaze: Melt the remaining 6 tablespoons of butter in a small saucepan over low heat. Add the honey and salt and stir until the mixture is thoroughly blended. Remove it from the heat, stir in the orange juice and pour it over the sweet potatoes. Sprinkle the potatoes with the poppy seeds, and bake them in a preheated 450° oven for 15 to 20 minutes, basting them with the glaze every 5 minutes. Just before serving, heat the rum, then pour it over the sweet potatoes. Ignite it and carry the flaming dish to the table.

Serves 6 to 8.

STEAMED 'KAMADA' SQUASH

ELEEN AUVIL BROGAN

2 tablespoons butter, softened
1 pound summer squash or zucchini, cut into ½-inch slices
2 tablespoons finely chopped fresh dill

In the center of a 2-foot square of heavy duty aluminum foil, smear an 8-inch square section with 1 tablespoon of the softened butter. Mound the squash on it and sprinkle it with the dill. Dot with the remaining tablespoon of butter.

Bring 2 opposing corners of the square together and fold them over each other 2 or 3 times to seal them completely. Fold the 2 remaining ends of foil over the sealed corners in such a fashion as to make a package that is as airtight as possible.

Bake the wrapped squash in a preheated 400° oven for 45 to 50 minutes. Unwrap and test the vegetables to see if they are tender; if not, rewrap and steam them 10 minutes longer.

Serves 4.

Editors' comments: *A "kamada" is a Japanese charcoal-fueled ceramic baking oven. Because such an oven is not readily available, we took Mrs. Brogan's interesting and original cooking method and adapted it to our Western ovens. This cooking method is equally successful with any vegetable that has a high water content: onions, celery, mushrooms, green peppers, eggplants. They may be cooked separately or in combination. It does not work, however, with members of the bean or pea family whose water content is minimal. Do not salt the vegetables as salt draws out their juices and impairs the steaming process.*

GARDEN VEGETABLE CASSEROLE

ANN KRESTENSEN

¼ cup olive oil
1 teaspoon finely chopped garlic
3 large onions, thinly sliced
¾ cup sliced celery
3 seeded and julienned large green peppers
5 medium-sized zucchini, unpeeled and cut into
    ½-inch slices
5 large tomatoes, peeled and sliced
2 fresh basil leaves, minced, or 1 teaspoon dried basil
½ teaspoon oregano
1½ teaspoons salt
½ teaspoon freshly ground black pepper

In a 3- to 4-quart flame-proof casserole heat the oil, then drop in the garlic and onions. Sauté, stirring frequently, until the vegetables are soft and somewhat translucent, about 5 minutes. Add the celery and green peppers and cook, stirring constantly, 5 minutes longer. Finally, add the zucchini and tomatoes, the basil, oregano, salt and pepper. Stir well to combine the ingredients.

Cover the casserole, lower the heat, and simmer until the vegetables are tender, about 20 minutes. Serve immediately, or reheat just before serving.

Serves 6 to 8.

RATATOUILLE NIÇOISE

CAROLYN KRIEGMAN

4 tablespoons olive oil
1 cup coarsely chopped onions
2 teaspoons finely chopped garlic
1 medium-sized zucchini or summer squash, washed
    and cut into ¼-inch slices
3 large, ripe tomatoes, peeled and cut into ⅓-inch slices
    One 1-pound eggplant, peeled and cut into
    ⅓-inch slices
1 seeded and julienned large green pepper
2 teaspoons salt
½ teaspoon freshly ground black pepper
1 teaspoon curry powder

In a 4- to 5-quart flame-proof casserole, heat 3 tablespoons
of the olive oil, then sauté the onions and 1 teaspoon of
the garlic until they are soft. Remove the casserole from
the heat and arrange the sliced vegetables in it in layers,
ending with a layer of tomatoes and sprinkling the
remaining teaspoon of garlic, the salt, pepper and curry
powder evenly between the layers. Pour the remaining
tablespoon of olive oil over the contents of the casserole.
Cover, and gently simmer the casserole over a low
flame for 30 minutes, or until the vegetables are tender.

Serves 4 to 6.

SNOW PEAS, WATER CHESTNUTS AND MUSHROOMS

BARBARA SHAWCROFT

5 tablespoons butter
5 tablespoons soy oil
1 pound mushrooms, thinly sliced
1½ pounds fresh snow peas, strings removed, or three 7-ounce boxes frozen snow peas, thoroughly defrosted
One 8½-ounce can water chestnuts, drained and thinly sliced
½ cup chicken stock, plus 2 tablespoons chicken stock
½ teaspoon ground fennel
2 tablespoons sake
3 tablespoons rice flour, or 3 tablespoons cornstarch
½ teaspoon salt
¼ teaspoon freshly ground black pepper

In a 12- to 14-inch skillet, heat the butter and oil until the butter foams. Add the mushrooms and sauté until their liquid has evaporated. Drop in the snow peas and water chestnuts and ½ cup of the chicken stock, bring to a boil and cook, covered, over medium heat until the peas are just tender, about 2 minutes.

Meanwhile, in a small bowl, combine the remaining 2 tablespoons of chicken stock with the fennel, sake, rice flour, salt and pepper and stir to form a smooth paste. Pour it over the peas, and mix thoroughly. Cook, stirring constantly for 2 or 3 minutes, until the sauce has thickened slightly. Serve immediately.

Serves 8.

BULGUR WITH BROCCOLI AND TOMATOES

KARA LANG

3 tablespoons salad oil
1 teaspoon finely chopped garlic
2 cups bulgur (cracked wheat)
4 cups chicken stock or water
1 cup finely chopped broccoli heads (stems removed)
12 to 18 cherry tomatoes
½ cup grated sharp cheddar cheese
½ cup toasted sesame seeds*

In a flame-proof casserole, heat the oil, then add the chopped garlic and the bulgur and stir until the bulgur is slightly toasted and thoroughly coated with the oil. Pour in the chicken stock or water, then bring the liquid to a boil, cover and simmer over low heat for 25 to 30 minutes, or until there is about ¼ inch, or less, of liquid covering the bulgur.

Without combining them with the bulgur, distribute the chopped broccoli and cherry tomatoes evenly over the surface of the casserole. Cover and simmer 10 minutes longer. At this point, the stock should have been completely absorbed by the bulgur, and the broccoli and tomatoes should be cooked but crisp. If not, cook 5 minutes longer. Then add the grated cheese. Turn off the heat and replace the cover to melt the cheese. This will take about 5 minutes.

Sprinkle the toasted sesame seeds over the casserole and serve immediately.

Serves 4 to 6.

*See index

BAKED TOMATOES STUFFED WITH MUSHROOMS

BARBARA SHAWCROFT

4 large, ripe tomatoes
4 tablespoons butter, plus 1 teaspoon butter
½ pound mushrooms, thinly sliced
½ cup sour cream
2 teaspoons flour
1 ounce bleu cheese
¼ teaspoon dried mixed salad herbs
½ teaspoon finely chopped parsley
1 tablespoon dry sherry
½ teaspoon salt
¼ teaspoon freshly ground black pepper
1 tablespoon sesame seeds, toasted*
½ teaspoon paprika

Remove and discard ½ inch from the top of each tomato. With a teaspoon, carefully scoop out the tomato pulp and reserve it for another use. Invert the tomato shells on a wire rack to drain.

In a 10-inch skillet melt the 4 tablespoons of butter and when it foams drop in the sliced mushrooms and sauté over medium heat for 10 to 15 minutes until they are soft and their juices have evaporated.

As the mushrooms are cooking, combine the sour cream and flour in a small bowl, stirring to prevent the flour from lumping. Add the bleu cheese, mixed salad herbs, parsley, sherry, salt and pepper and blend thoroughly. Add the sour cream mixture to the cooked mushrooms in the skillet and cook for 3 to 5 minutes, until the sauce thickens and bubbles. Remove from the stove and cool.

Spoon the cooled mixture into the tomato shells. Place them in a baking dish which has been greased with the remaining teaspoon of butter and sprinkle some of the toasted sesame seeds and paprika on each stuffed tomato. Bake in a preheated 375° oven for 15 to 25 minutes, until the tomatoes are soft and the filling is sizzling.

Serves 4.

*See index

BAKED SOY BEANS

PRISCILLA MERRITT

2 cups dried soy beans, thoroughly rinsed and any
   discolored beans discarded
6 to 8 cups water
⅔ cup dark, unsulfured molasses
1 tablespoon sea salt
2 to 3 celery stalks, each broken into 3 pieces
1 large onion, peeled and quartered
¼ cup olive oil

Drop the soy beans into a bean pot or a heavy oven-proof casserole equipped with a tightly fitting lid. Pour in water to cover the beans by at least 1½ to 2 inches. Soak overnight.

Without draining the liquid from the pot, add the molasses, sea salt, celery, onions and olive oil and mix well. Cover tightly, then bake in a preheated 225° oven for 7 hours, stirring occasionally. Remove the lid and bake 1 hour longer.

Serves 6 to 8.

RED BEANS AND RICE

WILHELMINA GODFREY

¾ cup small red kidney beans, or one 1-pound can red kidney beans, drained
3 teaspoons salt
1 cup white rice
¼ pound salt pork, cut into ¼-inch dice
1 teaspoon finely chopped garlic
½ cup coarsely chopped onions
¼ cup coarsely chopped green pepper
1 large tomato, peeled and diced
½ teaspoon freshly ground black pepper
4 or 5 drops Tabasco or to taste

If you are using the uncooked, dried beans, rinse them well and bring them to a boil in a 2- to 3-quart saucepan with 1 teaspoon of the salt and 5 cups of water. Partially cover the saucepan and simmer for 1½ hours, or until the beans are tender. Drain and reserve the beans.

Meanwhile, in another 2- to 3-quart saucepan, bring 6 cups of water to a boil. Add 1 teaspoon of the remaining salt and the rice slowly so that the water boils without interruption. Cook the rice, uncovered, over medium heat for 20 to 25 minutes, or until it is just tender. Drain and add the rice to the cooked or canned beans, gently tossing them with a fork.

In a 10- to 12-inch skillet, fry the salt pork dice until the fat is rendered and the pork is crisp. Remove the dice with a slotted spoon and drain them on paper towels. Fry the garlic, onions and green pepper in the rendered pork fat until they are soft. Then add the diced tomato and cook until the liquid has evaporated, about 5 minutes. Add the rice-and-beans, 1 teaspoon of salt, the pepper and Tabasco. Toss to mix well. Cover the skillet and steam about 5 minutes. Serve immediately, garnished with the drained pork bits.

Serves 4 to 6.

HERBED RICE

ADELA AKERS

3 tablespoons butter
1 cup finely chopped onions
1 cup brown rice
½ teaspoon dried marjoram
½ teaspoon dried summer savory
1 teaspoon dried rosemary, crushed with a mortar and pestle
1 teaspoon salt
2 cups chicken stock or 2 cups water

In a flame-proof casserole or a 2- to 3-quart casserole, melt the butter and when it foams drop in the onions and rice. Stir until the onions are translucent, then add the marjoram, summer savory, rosemary and salt. Mix well. Pour in the stock, bring it to a boil, reduce the heat and cover tightly. Simmer 40 to 45 minutes, or until the rice is tender but still crunchy. Serve directly from the casserole, or transfer to a heated serving dish.

Serves 4 to 6.

BAKED RICE

HERBERT COHEN

¼ cup butter
3 tablespoons finely chopped onion
1 cup long grained rice
2 cups beef stock
¼ cup sliced black pitted olives
⅓ cup sliced pimientos, drained

In a 2- to 3-quart flame-proof casserole, melt the butter and, when it foams, sauté the onions for 1 to 2 minutes until they are just soft. Add the rice and, stirring frequently, cook about 5 minutes until it has absorbed some of the butter and the grains are shiny. Pour in the beef stock, stirring once or twice to separate the rice grains, then add the olives and pimientos. Bring the liquid to a rapid boil. Cover the casserole and bake in a preheated 275° oven for 1 hour, or until the rice is tender.

Serves 4.

BAKED BROWN RICE

BILL SAX

3 tablespoons butter
1 cup coarsely chopped onions
4 teaspoons finely chopped garlic
1 cup brown rice
2 cups beef or vegetable stock

In a 2-quart flame-proof casserole, melt the butter. When it is foaming, sauté the onions until they are soft and translucent. Raise the heat to medium-high and add the garlic and brown rice.

Meanwhile, in a small saucepan, heat the beef or vegetable stock to the boiling point.

When the rice begins to toast, stir it constantly to brown all the grains without burning them. When the rice is uniformly brown and the stock is boiling, pour the liquid over the rice and stir. Cover the casserole and bake the rice in a preheated 325° oven for 40 minutes. Uncover the dish and bake an additional 10 minutes. Serve immediately.

Serves 4.

PILAF

PAULA GOLLHARDT

3 tablespoons olive oil
1 cup finely chopped onions
1 teaspoon finely chopped garlic
1 teaspoon curry powder
2 cups long grain converted rice
2 teaspoons salt
4 cups beef stock
½ cup seedless raisins or currants
½ cup blanched, slivered almonds
3 tablespoons finely chopped parsley

In a flame-proof casserole, heat the olive oil and, over a low flame, sauté the onions and garlic until they are translucent and soft. Add the curry powder and cook a few minutes longer to develop the curry flavor and color the onions deep yellow. Drop in the rice, mixing well to coat each grain with oil. Sprinkle in the salt and, finally, add the beef stock. Bring the liquid to a boil and stir to make certain that no rice sticks to the bottom of the casserole. Cover, reduce the heat and simmer about 20 minutes.

When the rice is nearly tender, add the raisins or currants, the almonds and parsley. Mix well. Cover and simmer 5 minutes longer, or until the rice is cooked and the raisins are plump.

Serves 6 to 8.

BAKED NOODLES

MARY NYBURG

1 teaspoon butter
3 cups fine egg noodles
1 cup cottage cheese
1 cup sour cream, plus ½ cup (optional)
1 teaspoon finely chopped garlic
1 tablespoon Worcestershire sauce
1 dash Tabasco
½ teaspoon salt
¼ teaspoon white pepper
2 tablespoons grated Parmesan cheese

Grease an oven-proof casserole with the butter. In a large pot of salted, boiling water cook the noodles for 3 minutes. Drain and run cold water over the noodles. Transfer them to the casserole.

In a small bowl, blend the cottage cheese with one cup of the sour cream. Stir in the garlic, Worcestershire sauce, Tabasco, salt and pepper and pour the mixture over the noodles, mixing well. Cover the casserole and bake in a preheated 350° oven for 45 minutes. Uncover, and sprinkle the Parmesan cheese over the casserole, then bake it 10 minutes longer, or until the top is delicately browned. Present the casserole with the optional ½ cup of sour cream in a separate bowl.

Serves 4 to 6.

HOME-GROWN SPROUTS

EDITORS

2 tablespoons alfalfa seeds, or mung beans
Water

Place the alfalfa seeds or mung beans in the bottom of a 1-quart Mason jar equipped with a screw-type lid. Cover the jar with a double thickness of cheesecloth and secure it with an elastic band or the outside metal rim of the screw-top. The cheesecloth will act as both a strainer and an air screen.

Cover the seeds with tepid water and let them soak for 6 to 8 hours. Drain off the soaking liquid, rinse the seeds, and drain them well. Cover the jar with a terry cloth towel and place it on its side in an out-of-the-way spot in your kitchen. Repeat the watering and draining procedure twice daily, covering the jar each time. The seeds should be neither too wet nor too dry or they will spoil. In a few days the seeds will swell and sprout. When they are fully sprouted, set the jar in the refrigerator, tightly covered, and use as needed.

(The green "shells" of the mung beans may be removed after sprouting, if desired, by rinsing the sprouts under a strong spray of cold water until the shells float free.)

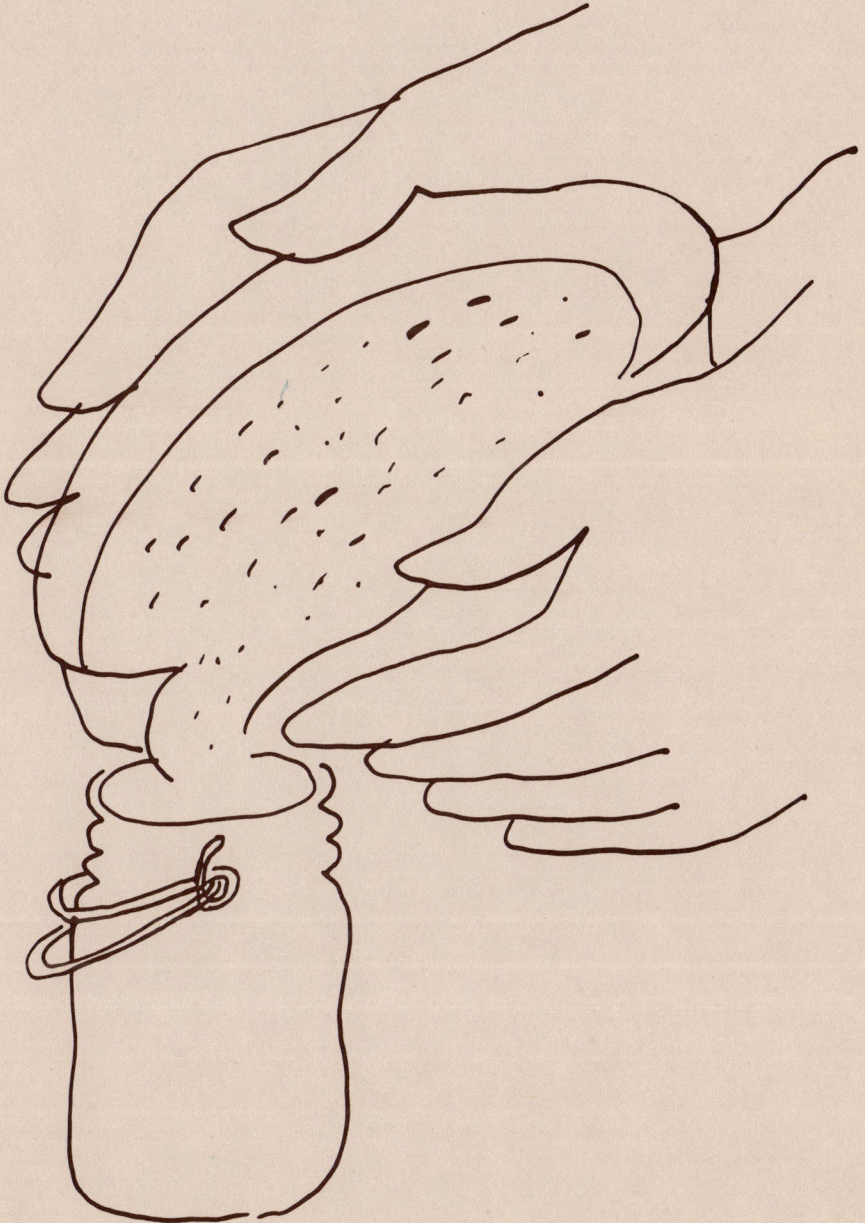

CURRIED CRANBERRY WALNUT RELISH

ADELA AKERS

4 cups fresh cranberries, about 1 pound
2 cups sugar
2 cups water
1 cup coarsely chopped walnuts
1 teaspoon curry powder
2 tablespoons chopped mango chutney

Pick over the cranberries and discard any soft or moldy fruit.

In a 3- to 4-quart saucepan, combine the sugar and water and stir until the sugar has dissolved. Bring the liquid to a boil, lower the heat and boil for 5 minutes. Add the cranberries and cook them 15 minutes. Remove from the heat and stir in the walnuts, curry powder and chopped chutney. Pour the relish into a mold or serving bowl. Cool and refrigerate.

Yield: 4 cups

PEACH CHUTNEY

BRYN KELSEY

1 pound peaches, peeled, sliced and cut into ½-inch dice
1 large apple, peeled, cored and cut into ½-inch dice
1½ cups finely chopped celery
1 sweet red pepper, seeded and cut into ½-inch dice
1 cup water
1 cup seedless raisins
1½ cups cider vinegar
2 cups sugar
1 teaspoon salt

In a medium-sized saucepan combine the peaches, apple, celery, pepper and ½ cup of the water. Cook over low heat until the ingredients are soft, about 10 to 15 minutes. Meanwhile, in a smaller saucepan, pour the remaining ½ cup of water over the raisins, partially cover the pan, and cook over low heat for 20 minutes. Set aside.

Add the vinegar, sugar and salt to the peach-and-apple mixture and stir over medium to high heat until the sugar is dissolved. Continue to cook for about 45 minutes, or until the mixture is thick and almost transparent. Stir occasionally to prevent burning. Mix in the reserved raisins and pour the chutney into sterilized jars.

Yield: 2 pints

TOMATO SAMBAL

MEL SOMEROSKI

⅔ cup finely chopped red onions
⅔ cup peeled anh finely chopped tomatoes
⅔ cup peeled, seeded and finely chopped cucumbers
    (see Chilled Yoghurt-Cucumber Soup)
 2 tablespoons lime juice
¼ teaspoon salt

In a small bowl gently toss together the chopped onions, tomatoes and cucumbers. Sprinkle the lime juice and salt over the vegetables and toss again.

Refrigerate for at least one hour before serving. Serve with curry dishes or Chicken Buriyani*.

Yield: 2 cups

DILL PICKLES

HOWARD KOTTLER

For each quart jar:

Four to six 4-inch pickling cucumbers
1 tablespoon salt
1 tablespoon pickling spices
1 sprig fresh dill weed
1 to 4 garlic cloves, according to taste
½ hot chili pepper, seeded
Boiling water

If possible, select hard cucumbers that have been picked recently. Wash them and soak them in salted cold water for at least 2 hours.

Sterilize quart jars and lids by setting them in an 8- to 10-quart kettle filled with water. Cover the pot, bring the water to a boil, and boil 20 minutes. With tongs, remove the jars from the pot and immediately pack them with as many cucumbers as can be comfortably accommodated in each jar. Sprinkle 1 tablespoon of salt and 1 tablespoon of pickling spices into each jar, wedge in the dill sprig, garlic cloves and chili pepper, and fill it with boiling water. Seal immediately with sterilized lids.

TOASTED SESAME SEEDS

ANNA KANG BURGESS

2 cups sesame seeds
1 teaspoon salt

In a heavy 10-inch skillet, toast the sesame seeds over low heat, stirring constantly, until they turn delicately brown. Sprinkle in the salt, then, with the back of a spoon, mash the seeds slightly.

Yield: 2 cups

Editors' comments: *Stored in a tightly sealed jar in the refrigerator, toasted sesame seeds can be kept for several months.*

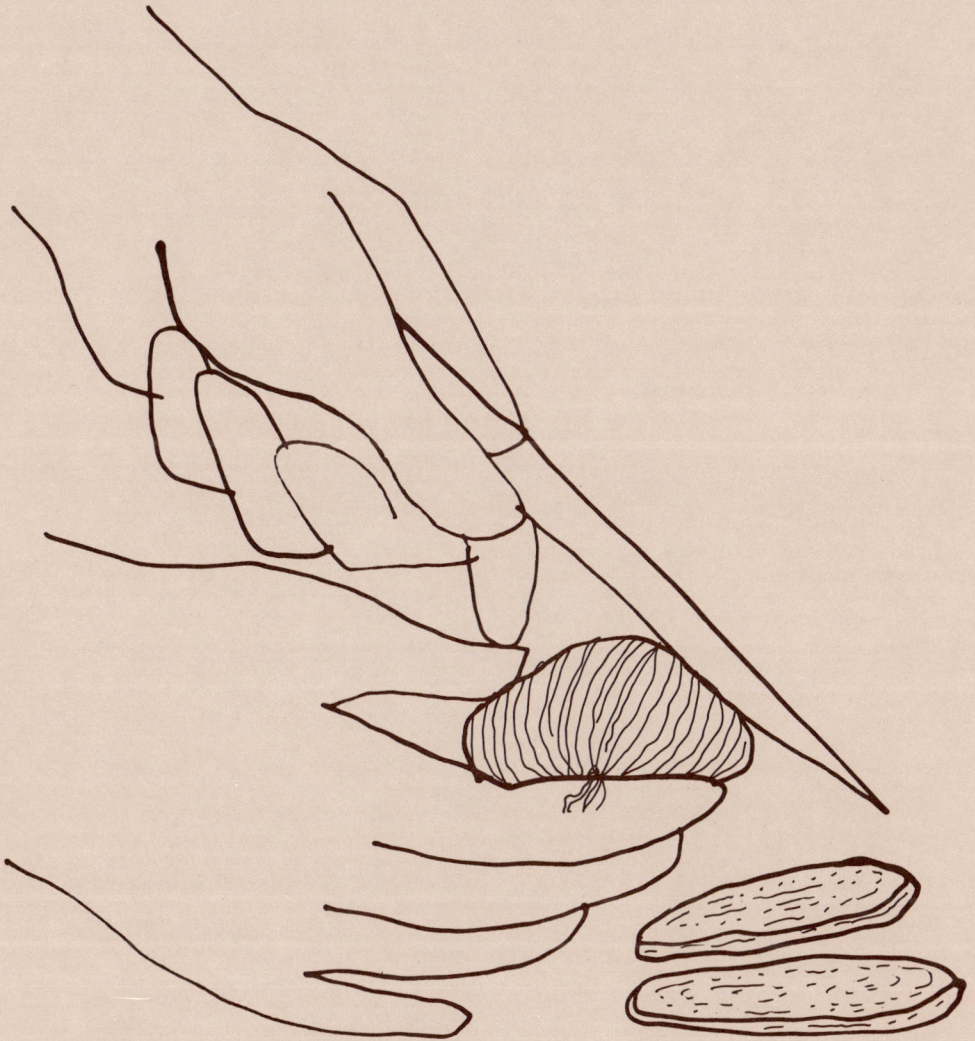

GREEK SALAD

MARILYN PAPPAS

1 large head Boston lettuce or about 12 cups
    mixed greens
½ cup thinly sliced scallions, including 2 inches of
    green tops
¼ cup finely chopped parsley
4 large radishes, thinly sliced
1 large green pepper, seeded and cut into ½-inch dice
1 large cucumber, peeled, seeded and cut into ¼-inch dice
1 or 2 tomatoes, cut into wedges
    Half a 2-ounce can anchovies
2 teaspoons capers, rinsed and drained
12 black Greek olives
    6 canned, medium-hot chili peppers (pepperettes), halved
¼ pound Feta cheese, crumbled

Dressing:
½ cup olive oil
¼ cup wine vinegar
1 teaspoon lemon juice
1 teaspoon finely chopped garlic
½ teaspoon salt
¼ teaspoon freshly ground black pepper
½ teaspoon oregano

Thoroughly wash and drain the lettuce or greens, discarding any bruised or discolored leaves, then tear it into bite-sized pieces.

To dry them, pat the pieces with paper towels. Place them in a large salad bowl and add the scallions, parsley, radishes, green pepper, cucumber, tomatoes, anchovies, capers, olives, chili peppers and cheese. Toss to distribute the ingredients evenly. Refrigerate until ready to serve.

To make the dressing: Combine the oil, vinegar, lemon juice, garlic, salt, pepper and oregano in a small bowl or jar, and stir or shake until the ingredients are thoroughly blended. Pour the dressing over the salad and toss well to coat the leaves. Serve immediately.

Serves 4 to 6.

'MIXED MEDIA' SALAD

JAMIE BENNETT

½ head escarole (6 cups)
½ head iceberg lettuce (8 cups)
½ pound spinach
2 tablespoons finely minced pimientos
½ cup thinly sliced black pitted olives
1 medium-sized onion, thinly sliced
1 tablespoon finely chopped parsley

Dressing:
¾ cup salad oil
1 teaspoon oregano
1 tablespoon dried basil
¼ teaspoon dry mustard
½ teaspoon Worcestershire sauce
1 teaspoon salt
¼ teaspoon freshly ground black pepper
1 teaspoon finely chopped garlic
¼ cup wine vinegar
2 tablespoons lemon juice

Thoroughly wash and drain the escarole, lettuce and spinach, discarding any bruised or discolored leaves and the tough spinach stems. Tear the greens into bite-sized pieces. To dry them, pat the pieces with paper towels, then place them in a salad bowl and refrigerate them until you are ready to serve.

Meanwhile, mix the dressing by combining the salad oil, oregano, basil, mustard and Worcestershire sauce, salt and pepper in a small bowl or jar and stir or shake until the salt has dissolved and the mustard is absorbed. Add the garlic, vinegar and lemon juice and mix thoroughly.

At serving-time, remove the greens from the refrigerator and sprinkle in the pimientos, olives and onions. Stir or shake the dressing and pour it over the salad. Toss vigorously to coat the leaves, then garnish with the parsley.

Serves 4 to 6.

POLISH ZUCCHINI

FRANÇOISE GROSSEN

4 small zucchini, peeled
1¼ teaspoons salt
¼ cup olive oil
4 teaspoons wine vinegar
¼ teaspoon dry English mustard
   Pinch of freshly ground black pepper
1 tablespoon finely chopped scallions
1 tablespoon chopped parsley

Split the zucchini in half lengthwise. In a 2- to 3-quart saucepan, bring some water to a boil and add 1 teaspoon of the salt. Drop in the zucchini and simmer, partially covered, for 7 to 10 minutes, or until they are tender. Drain them and set aside to cool.

The zucchini may be served chilled or at room temperature. To make the dressing: In a small bowl or jar, combine the olive oil, vinegar, mustard, the remaining ¼ teaspoon of salt, and the pepper and stir or shake vigorously until they are thoroughly blended. Pour the dressing over the zucchini, then sprinkle them with the scallions and parsley.

Serve as an hors d'oeuvre or salad.

Serves 4.

Editors' comment: *The success of this dish depends on the size and freshness of the zucchini. Old or large zucchini should not be used.*

RAITA (INDIAN CUCUMBER AND YOGHURT SALAD)

SUSAN WEITZMAN

1 teaspoon ground cumin
¼ teaspoon crushed red pepper
1 teaspoon salt
1 pint yoghurt (unflavored)
1 ripe avocado, peeled and cut into ½-inch cubes
1 teaspoon lemon juice
½ cup thinly sliced scallions
2 cucumbers, peeled, seeded, and coarsely grated
½ cup seeded and coarsely chopped green peppers
3 tablespoons finely chopped Chinese parsley

In a small skillet, toast the ground cumin and crushed red pepper over very low heat for 1 to 2 minutes, stirring occasionally to develop their flavor. Then combine them with the salt and fold into the yoghurt.

Place the avocado cubes in a small salad bowl and sprinkle lemon juice over them. Add the scallions, grated cucumber, green peppers and Chinese parsley and toss to mix. Pour the yoghurt mixture over the vegetables and toss gently to coat them thoroughly. Refrigerate the raita to chill it thoroughly, at least 2 hours.

Serves 6.

SALADE DIABLE

JON B. WAHLING

5 slices bacon
1 garlic clove, peeled
1 teaspoon salt
3 tablespoons wine vinegar
  Dash Tabasco
1 teaspoon dry mustard
½ teaspoon freshly ground black pepper
½ cup olive oil
5 scallions, thinly sliced
2 hard-boiled eggs, mashed
  About 10 cups mixed salad greens, thoroughly
    washed and dried (watercress, Boston lettuce,
    iceberg lettuce, romaine, escarole, endive, etc.)

In a heavy skillet, sauté the bacon until it is crisp and slightly browned. Transfer the slices to drain on paper towels.

In a large wooden salad bowl, vigorously mash the garlic clove with the back of a spoon, rubbing it against all inside surfaces of the bowl before discarding it. Add the salt and vinegar and mix until the salt is dissolved. Then add the Tabasco, mustard and pepper, stirring to blend the mustard. Mix in the olive oil and stir. Then, drop in the sliced scallions and the mashed eggs. Finally, add the greens, tossing them to thoroughly coat the leaves with the dressing. Crumble the bacon over the salad.

Serves 6.

SPINACH AND ORANGE SALAD

ARLINE FISCH

4 large navel oranges, peeled and sliced
2 medium-sized onions, peeled and thinly sliced
One 10-ounce package fresh spinach, or 1½ pounds garden spinach, washed and dried
¼ pound mushrooms, thinly sliced

Dressing:
⅓ cup olive oil
⅓ cup wine vinegar
1 teaspoon sugar
½ teaspoon salt
¼ teaspoon chili powder
¼ teaspoon freshly ground black pepper

In a small bowl or jar, combine the oil, vinegar, sugar, salt, chili powder and pepper. Stir or shake until the sugar is dissolved and the ingredients are thoroughly blended.

In a medium-sized bowl, arrange the orange slices alternately with the onions. Add the dressing and toss. Refrigerate 2 to 3 hours.

At serving time pick over the spinach and discard all stems and any wilted leaves. Add the marinated orange and onion slices and top with the sliced mushrooms. Toss well to coat all the spinach with the dressing. Serve immediately.

Serves 6 to 8.

SPINACH SALAD

MYRA BUCHNER

½ pound fresh spinach
6 slices bacon
1 tablespoon salad oil
½ cup tarragon vinegar
¼ teaspoon salt
¼ teaspoon freshly ground black pepper

Several hours before serving the salad, thoroughly wash and drain the spinach. Tear off and discard the tough stems, along with any bruised leaves. Pat the spinach dry with paper towels and place it in a salad bowl in the refrigerator.

Just before serving, cook the bacon until it is crisp and transfer it to paper towels to drain. In a small saucepan combine the oil, vinegar, salt and pepper and heat the mixture, stirring occasionally, until the salt has dissolved.

Pour the dressing over the spinach and toss the salad. Crumble the bacon over the greens and toss again.

Serves 4.

Editors' comments: *Because the vinegar dominates this dressing, it should be a particularly flavorful type.*

SUNOMONO (JAPANESE CUCUMBER SALAD)

KAY SEKIMACHI

1 large cucumber
½ teaspoon salt
3 tablespoons white wine vinegar
2 tablespoons sugar
½ teaspoon monosodium glutamate
1 teaspoon peeled and thinly sliced fresh ginger root
¼ cup finely chopped cooked shrimp or crab meat

Peel the cucumber, retaining alternate green strips of skin for color. Chop off the ends. Cut the cucumber in half lengthwise and, with the tip of a spoon, scrape out and discard the seeds. Cut the cucumber diagonally into thin slices, then place the slices in a small bowl and sprinkle with ¼ teaspoon of the salt. Toss well and set the bowl aside for at least 30 minutes.

Meanwhile, prepare the dressing: Combine the vinegar, sugar, monosodium glutamate and the remaining ¼ teaspoon of salt, and stir until the dry ingredients are dissolved. Drain the cucumber, pressing the slices to release all their liquid. Add the sliced ginger root to the cucumber and pour in the dressing, then toss.

Serve in small individual bowls and garnish with the shrimp or crab meat.

Serves 4.

TABBOULEH (ARABIC SALAD)

SAM MALOOF

¼ cup bulgur (cracked wheat)
¾ cup finely chopped scallions, including 2 inches of green tops
2 cups finely chopped parsley
¾ cup finely chopped fresh mint
4 large tomatoes, peeled and cut into ½-inch dice
½ cup olive oil
1 teaspoon salt
¼ teaspoon freshly ground black pepper
Pinch of cayenne (optional)
2 tablespoons lemon juice

Set the bulgur in a small bowl and pour boiling water over it to cover it by 1 inch. Soak the bulgur at least one hour, preferably two. Drain well.

In a salad bowl, toss the scallions, parsley, mint and tomatoes to mix them well. Add the drained bulgur and toss again. Then add the oil, salt, pepper and cayenne, if you are using it, and pour in the lemon juice. Stir the tabbouleh to mix it thoroughly.

Serves 6 to 8.

Editors' comments: *Serve this dish as an hors d'oeuvre on pieces of Lebanese—or Syrian—bread. Or it may be presented on a side plate nesting in romaine leaves.*

Accompanying dishes:
Craftsman: rice, Shaykh el Mekshey, Lebanese bread

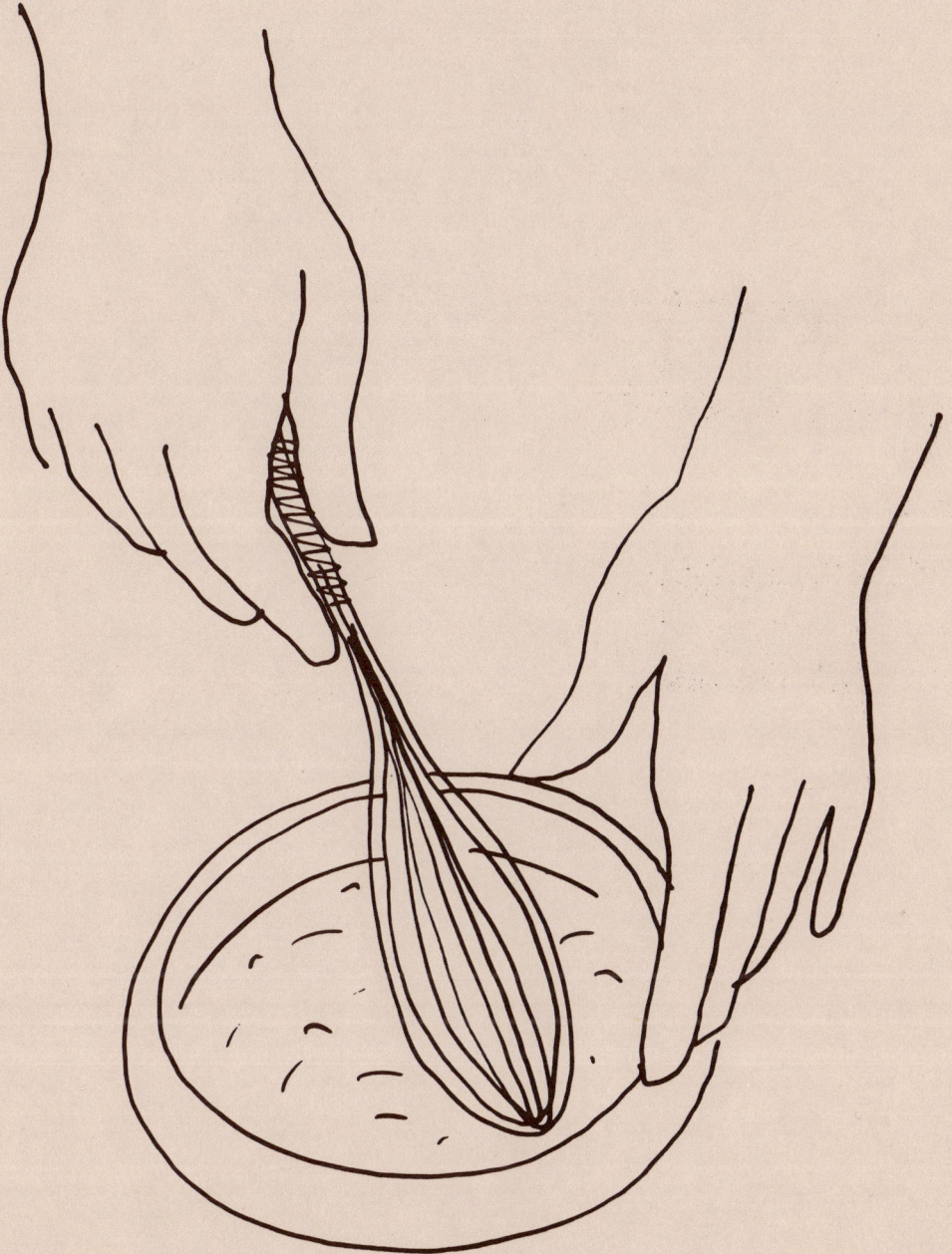

DESSERTS

BUTTERED RUM PEACHES

VIVIKA HEINO

1½ cups sugar
3 cups water
8 ripe peaches, peeled, pitted and halved
8 teaspoons dark brown sugar
4 teaspoons butter
½ cup Jamaican rum
1 cup heavy cream, whipped

In a 3- to 4-quart saucepan, combine the sugar and water and stir them over medium heat until the sugar is dissolved. Bring the mixture to a boil, then lower the heat so the syrup is barely simmering and gently lower the peach halves into the syrup. Partially cover the saucepan, and cook, over low heat, for 5 minutes, or until the peaches are just tender. Immediately, transfer the peaches with a slotted spoon to an oven-proof baking dish, placing them cut side up. Raise the heat under the saucepan and briskly boil its contents until the syrup is reduced by half.

Place ½ teaspoon of dark brown sugar in each peach half and dot it with ¼ teaspoon of the butter. Combine 1 cup of the peach syrup with the rum and carefully pour the mixture into baking dish. Bake the peaches in a preheated 350° oven for 15 minutes. Serve warm, topped with the whipped cream.

Serves 8.

Editors' comments: *Canned peach halves may be substituted if fresh peaches are unavailable.*

CARROT CAKE

JANE BROWN

1 teaspoon butter
1½ cups salad oil
2 cups sugar
4 eggs
1 teaspoon salt
1 tablespoon cinnamon
2 cups flour
2 teaspoons baking soda
3 cups grated carrots (about 1½ pounds)
1 cup blanched and finely chopped almonds, or
    substitute walnuts

Grease a 10-inch tube cake pan with the butter.

Blend the oil and sugar together in a large bowl with a wooden spoon. Add the eggs, one at a time, beating well after each addition. In another bowl, sift together the salt, cinnamon, flour and baking soda. Add the sifted ingredients to the egg mixture, and stir until they are thoroughly incorporated. Next, beat in the carrots and almonds and mix them to blend thoroughly.

Pour the batter into the prepared cake pan and bake it in a preheated 325° oven for 1¼ hours, or until a knife inserted in the center of the cake comes out clean.

Cream Cheese Icing
    One 8-ounce package cream cheese, softened
¼ cup butter, melted
2 tablespoons vanilla
    One 1-pound box confectioners' sugar

With an electric mixer, beat the cream cheese until it is light and fluffy. Gradually add the melted butter, beating until it is completely absorbed. Add the vanilla and the sugar, beating well after each addition so that the icing is smooth.

Remove the cooled cake from the pan, then smooth the icing over the top and sides.

Yield: One 10 inch cake

CHEESECAKE

MYRA BUCHNER

Crust:
  A 6-ounce box zwieback
  ½ cup butter, melted
1¼ cups sugar
  ½ teaspoon cinnamon

Filling:
  5 eggs
    Three 8-ounce packages cream cheese, softened
  1 cup sugar
  1 teaspoon vanilla

Topping:
  ¾ cup sour cream
  3 tablespoons sugar
  1 teaspoon vanilla

To make the crust: Crush the zwieback with a rolling pin until they are finely ground. In a bowl combine the crumbs, melted butter, sugar and cinnamon. Mix until the butter is thoroughly distributed and the crumbs are slightly moist. Press the mixture into a 9-inch spring-form pan, molding it evenly over the bottom and lower two inches of the pan. Refrigerate for ½ hour until the crust is set.

To make the filling: In a electric blender, blend the eggs for 5 seconds. Add the softened cream cheese, a chunk at a time, and blend until smooth. Then add the sugar and vanilla and blend 10 seconds longer. Pour the contents of the blender into the chilled crust and bake in a preheated 350° oven for 50 minutes.

To make the topping: In a bowl thoroughly combine the sour cream, sugar and vanilla. Carefully spread the topping on the baked cheesecake with a rubber spatula and bake an additional 10 minutes. Remove from the oven, cool, then refrigerate at least 2 hours before serving.

Serves 8 to 12.

CHEESE TORTE

FRED ESCHER

Crust:
- 3 cups crushed graham crackers (about 40 crackers)
- 1 cup sugar
- 2 teaspoons cinnamon
- ½ cup butter, melted

Filling:
- 3 pounds dry (or diet) cottage cheese, small curd
- 2 cups sugar
- 2 cups heavy cream
- 6 eggs
- 2 teaspoons vanilla
- ½ cup flour, sifted

To make the crust: With a rolling pin, crush the crackers to a fine powder. In a large bowl, combine them with the sugar and cinnamon. Then pour the melted butter over the dry ingredients and mix well to moisten all the crumbs.

Press the mixture onto the bottom and sides of a 9-by-13-by-2-inch baking pan forming a uniformly even crust. Set the crust aside while you prepare the filling.

To make the filling: Place the cottage cheese, sugar, cream, eggs and vanilla in a large bowl. With an electric beater or mixer, beat them well; then, sprinkle in the sifted flour and continue beating hard for about five minutes, or until all the ingredients are thoroughly blended and almost smooth in texture. Pour the filling into the prepared crust and bake it in a preheated 350° oven for 1¼ hours, or until a knife inserted in the center of the filling comes out clean.

Yield: One 9 by 13 inch torte

SAMBUMBIA CAKE WITH PUDDING SAUCE

HERBERT COHEN

Cake:
- 2 teaspoons butter, softened
- 5 eggs
- 2 cups salad oil
- 2 cups sugar
- 1 tablespoon vanilla
- 1 tablespoon ground cinnamon
- 3 cups cake flour
- 1 tablespoon baking powder
- ½ teaspoon salt
- One 20-ounce can crushed pineapple, drained
- 1 pint fresh blueberries, or one 15-ounce can blueberries, drained
- 1 cup coarsely chopped pecans

Sauce:
- ½ cup butter
- 1 cup light brown sugar
- One 5¼ ounce can evaporated milk

To make the cake: Grease a 14-by-10-by-2-inch baking pan with the butter. In a large bowl, beat the eggs until they are light and frothy. Continue to beat while slowly adding in the oil and sugar. Then, stir in the vanilla and cinnamon.

Combine the cake flour, baking powder and salt and sift them into the egg-and-oil mixture. Add the crushed, drained pineapple, blueberries and pecans. Stir the batter gently to mix well.

Pour the batter into the prepared pan and bake it in a preheated 325° oven for 1 to 1¼ hours, or until a knife inserted in the center of the cake comes out clean. Set aside and cool.

To make the Pudding Sauce: In a small saucepan, over low heat, melt the ½ cup of butter, then add the brown sugar, and stir until it is dissolved. Slowly pour in the evaporated milk and mix until it is thoroughly blended. Bring the sauce to a boil over medium to high heat, reduce the heat, and cook for 5 minutes. Set aside to cool.

Present the cake in the baking dish with the thoroughly cooled sauce poured over it, or cut the cake into 2-inch squares and serve the sauce separately.

Yield: One 14 by 10 inch cake

FRESH PEACH COBBLER

VIRGINIA WEST

1 teaspoon butter, plus 2 tablespoons butter
⅔ cup sugar
2 tablespoons flour
½ teaspoon cinnamon
4 large peaches, peeled and cut into ½-inch slices, or
    3 cups of fresh fruit or berries

Batter:
⅓ cup butter, softened
1 egg, beaten
1 cup flour
2 tablespoons sugar
1½ teaspoons baking powder
½ teaspoon salt
3 tablespoons milk

Grease a 9-inch round cake pan with the teaspoon of butter. The cake pan should be at least 2 inches deep.

In a bowl, combine the sugar, flour and cinnamon. Drop in the peach slices and toss to coat them with the mixture. Arrange the peaches on the bottom of the prepared cake pan and dot them with the remaining 2 tablespoons of butter.

To make the batter: In a bowl, cream the butter until it is light and fluffy and then blend in the beaten egg. Combine the flour, sugar, baking powder and salt and sift them into the butter mixture alternately with the milk. With a rubber spatula, spread the batter over the peaches, distributing it as evenly as possible. Bake in a preheated 350° oven for 30 minutes.

Serve while the cobbler is still warm either with pouring cream or whipped cream.

Serves 6.

FRESH APPLE CAKE

FRED ESCHER

1 teaspoon butter, softened
1 cup sugar
½ cup salad oil
3 eggs
2 teaspoons vanilla
2 cups flour
1 teaspoon baking soda
1 teaspoon cinnamon
1 teaspoon salt
¼ cup milk
3 large apples, peeled, cored and cut into ¼-inch slices
½ cup coarsely chopped walnuts

Grease a 9-by-13-inch cake pan with the butter.

In a large bowl, combine the sugar and oil and mix them with a heavy wooden spoon until they are thoroughly blended. Then add the eggs, one at a time, beating well after each addition. Stir in the vanilla.

Combine the flour, baking soda, cinnamon and salt. Sift them into the sugar-and-egg mixture and beat well. Add the milk. Gently fold in the apples and walnuts, taking care not to crush the apples.

Pour the batter into the prepared cake pan and bake it in a preheated 350° oven for 40 to 45 minutes, or until a knife inserted in the center of the cake comes out clean. Remove the cake from the pan and cool it on a wire rack.

Yield: One 9 by 13 inch cake

SYLVIA'S APPLE CAKE

RUTH GINSBERG-PLACE

4 large apples, peeled and cut into ½ inch dice (4 cups)
2 cups sugar
1 cup coarsely chopped pecans
1 cup seedless raisins
1 teaspoon grated lemon rind
3 cups flour
½ teaspoon cinnamon
½ teaspoon salt
½ teaspoon baking soda
3 eggs
1 cup salad oil
1 teaspoon vanilla
1 teaspoon butter

In a large mixing bowl, toss together the apples, sugar, pecans, raisins and lemon rind. Set aside for 1 hour, stirring the apples occasionally. During this time the apples will release their juice, providing the liquid that is essential to the success of this cake.

Sift together the flour, cinnamon, salt and baking soda. In a separate bowl, beat the eggs well and continue to beat as you add the salad oil and vanilla. Pour the egg mixture into the sifted ingredients and combine thoroughly. The batter will be lumpy and somewhat sticky. Add the apples and stir vigorously to blend well. Pour the batter into a 9-inch round cake pan that has been greased with the teaspoon of butter and bake in a preheated 350° oven for 1½ hours, or until a knife inserted in the center of the cake comes out clean.

Yield: One 9 inch round cake

APPLESAUCE CAKE

RON KING

½ cup butter, softened, plus 1 teaspoon butter
1 cup light brown sugar
2 eggs
2 cups flour
½ teaspoon baking soda
1 teaspoon baking powder
1½ teaspoons salt
1 teaspoon cinnamon
½ teaspoon ground ginger
½ teaspoon ground cloves
1½ cups applesauce
¾ cup seedless raisins
Confectioners' sugar

In a large bowl, beat the butter and sugar until they are light and fluffy. Add the eggs, one at a time, beating well after each addition.

Sift together the flour, baking soda, baking powder, salt, cinnamon, ginger and cloves and add, alternately with the applesauce, to the egg mixture. Beat until well blended, then fold in the raisins.

Grease a 9-inch tube cake pan with the remaining teaspoon of butter and pour in the batter, spreading it evenly with a rubber spatula. Bake in a preheated 350° oven for 45 minutes, or until a knife inserted in the center of the cake comes out clean.

Transfer to a wire rack to cool and sprinkle with confectioners' sugar or a lemon or orange frosting of your choice.

Yield: One 9 inch round cake

ALMOND CRUSTY CAKE

RAGNHILD LANGLET

3 eggs
1⅓ cups sugar
2 teaspoons grated orange rind
½ teaspoon lemon extract
1 cup flour
½ teaspoon salt
1 teaspoon baking powder
⅓ cup orange juice
⅓ cup butter, melted, plus 1 tablespoon butter, softened
1 cup very finely chopped almonds
Confectioners' sugar (optional)

In a large bowl, beat the eggs. Gradually add the sugar and continue to beat until the mixture is thick and pale lemon-colored. Then, add the grated orange rind and the lemon extract.

Sift together the flour, salt and baking powder and add them to the egg mixture alternately with the orange juice. Pour in the melted butter and stir.

Grease a 9-inch Bundt cake pan with the remaining tablespoon of softened butter. Drop ¼ cup of the chopped almonds into the pan and, rolling and twisting the pan, coat it with the nuts. Use more of the nuts if necessary.

Add the remaining almonds to the batter and mix well. Pour the batter into the prepared Bundt pan and bake in a preheated 350° oven for 45 minutes, or until a knife inserted in the center of the cake comes out clean. Cool the cake before removing it from the pan.

Sprinkle the surface of the cake with the confectioners' sugar, if you like.

Yield: One 9 inch cake

EQUALITY CAKE

TRUDE GUERMONPREZ

1 teaspoon butter, softened, plus ¾ cup butter, softened
1 teaspoon flour
2 large eggs, separated, plus 1 large egg white
1 cup dark brown sugar
1 cup whole wheat flour
⅓ cup wheat germ
½ teaspoon salt
½ cup finely chopped walnuts
¼ cup blanched, slivered almonds
¼ cup pine nuts
⅔ cup seedless raisins
½ cup currants

Grease a 9-by-5-by-3-inch loaf pan with the teaspoon of softened butter, then dust it with the teaspoon of flour, and knock out any excess flour.

In a large bowl, beat the 3 egg whites until they are stiff, then refrigerate them.

In another large bowl, cream the remaining butter until it is light and fluffy. Gradually add the sugar, and beat well. Next, drop in the egg yolks, and mix until they are thoroughly blended. Combine the wheat flour, wheat germ and salt, and add them to the butter-and-sugar mixture, beating until all the flour has been thoroughly incorporated.

In a small bowl, combine the walnuts, almonds, pine nuts, raisins and currants and toss to mix them well. Stir ¼ of the cold egg whites into the batter with the nut mixture. Then, as gently as possible, fold the remaining stiffly beaten egg whites into the batter using a rubber spatula and an under-and-over motion.

Spoon the batter into the prepared loaf pan and, with the rubber spatula, smooth the surface. Bake in a preheated 350° oven for 1 hour, or until a knife inserted in the center of the cake comes out clean.

Yield: One 9 by 5 by 3 inch cake

Editors' comments: *This traditional recipe's name derives from the fact that the ingredients are measured according to their equivalent weights: flour, sugar, wheat germ and butter measurements are dictated by the weight of the eggs. Thus, it is important to use only large eggs, since smaller or larger eggs would throw the recipe off. For convenience, the original weight measurements have here been converted to cups.*

ROSE GERANIUM POUND CAKE

JOAN LINTAULT

1 teaspoon butter, softened, plus 1 cup butter, softened
20 rose geranium leaves, washed and patted dry with
    paper towels
1¼ cups sugar
5 eggs, lightly beaten
1 teaspoon vanilla
1 teaspoon finely grated lemon rind
1¾ cups flour
2 teaspoons baking powder
½ teaspoon salt
Confectioners' sugar

Grease the bottom and sides of a 9-by-5-by-3-inch loaf pan
with the teaspoon of softened butter. Carefully arrange
the rose geranium leaves around the bottom and sides
of the pan.

In a large bowl, beat the remaining cup of butter until it
is very light and fluffy. Gradually add the sugar while you
continue to beat, then pour in half the eggs and mix until
they are thoroughly blended. Add the remaining eggs along
with the vanilla and lemon rind and mix thoroughly.

In another bowl, sift together the flour, baking powder
and salt. Add the sifted ingredients to the butter mixture,
blending them well. Gently spoon the batter into the
prepared loaf pan, taking care not to disturb the leaves.
With a rubber spatula, spread the batter evenly in the pan
and smooth the surface. Bake in a preheated 325° oven
for 1 hour, or until a knife inserted in the center of the
cake comes out clean.

Remove the cake from the pan, invert it on a wire rack
and peel off any adhering leaves, then cool. Sprinkle with
the confectioners' sugar.

Yield: One 9 by 5 by 3 inch cake

NEVER-FAIL CHOCOLATE CAKE

PATRICK McCORMICK

1 teaspoon butter, softened, plus 2 tablespoons butter
Two 1-ounce squares semi-sweet chocolate
½ cup water
1 egg, well beaten
1 cup cake flour
1 cup sugar
¾ teaspoon baking soda
½ teaspoon salt
½ cup sour cream
1 tablespoon vanilla
Confectioners' sugar

Grease an 8-inch square cake pan with the teaspoon of softened butter.

Place the chocolate, the remaining 2 tablespoons of butter and the water in a double boiler and melt the butter and chocolate over rapidly boiling water. Then stir the mixture, remove it from the heat and set aside to cool. Beat in the egg.

Sift together the flour, sugar, baking soda and salt, and add them alternately with the sour cream to the chocolate mixture. When they are thoroughly blended, stir in the vanilla.

Pour the batter into the prepared cake pan and bake in a preheated 350° oven for 40 to 50 minutes, or until a knife inserted in the center of the cake comes out clean.

Remove the cake from the pan and cool it on a wire rack. Before serving dust with the confectioners' sugar.

Yield: One 8 by 8 inch cake

CHOCOLATE CHIP NUT CAKE

MARILYN PAPPAS

1 teaspoon butter, softened, plus 2 cups butter
1⅓ cups sugar
3 eggs
2¼ cups cake flour
2 teaspoons baking powder
½ teaspoon salt
¾ cup milk
1 teaspoon vanilla
2 cups finely chopped walnuts
One 6-ounce package chocolate chips

Grease a 9-inch tube cake pan with the teaspoon of softened butter.

In a large bowl, cream together the remaining 2 cups of butter and the sugar, until they are light and fluffy. One at a time, add the eggs, beating well after each addition.

Sift together twice the flour, baking powder and salt, then add them alternately with the milk to the butter-sugar mixture. Blend well. Add the vanilla and the chopped walnuts. Gently fold in the chocolate chips and pour the batter into the prepared cake pan. Bake in a preheated 325° oven for 1 hour, or until a knife inserted in the center of the cake comes out clean. Remove the cake from the pan and cool it on a wire rack.

Yield: One 9 inch tube cake

CHOCOLATE CREAM SPONGE CAKE

JUNE SCHWARCZ

Cake:

  2 teaspoons butter, softened
  2 teaspoons flour
  6 eggs, separated
  ½ teaspoon cream of tartar
  1 cup sugar
  2 teaspoons grated orange rind
  1 teaspoon almond extract
  1 cup cake flour
  ⅓ cup orange juice

Frosting:

  1 cup sweet butter, softened
  ½ cup confectioners' sugar
  ½ pound semi-sweet chocolate, melted and cooled
  3 eggs
    Pinch of salt
  ½ teaspoon vanilla

To make the cake: Grease each of two 9-inch cake pans with 1 teaspoon of the butter. (The pans should be at least 2 inches deep.) Place 1 teaspoon of the flour in each pan and, tipping and rolling the pan, dust it with the flour. Knock out any excess.

In a large bowl, beat the egg whites with the cream of tartar. Gradually add the sugar and continue to beat until the whites stand in stiff peaks.

In another bowl, beat the egg yolks until they are light and lemon-colored. Mix in the rind and almond extract. Add the flour alternately with the orange juice and beat until they are thoroughly blended.

Gently mix ¼ of the egg whites into the egg yolk mixture to lighten it. Then, fold the egg yolk mixture into the remaining egg whites. Divide the batter evenly between the two prepared cake pans and bake the cake in a preheated 325° oven for 25 minutes, or until a knife inserted in the center of the cake comes out clean. Cool before removing from the pans.

To make the frosting: Cream the butter and sugar together until they are soft and fluffy. Add the cooled chocolate, and mix well. Drop in the eggs, one at a time, beating well after each addition. Mix in the salt and vanilla.

160

When they are cool, remove the cakes from the pans and, with a bread knife, carefully cut each one in half horizontally, so as to end up with four layers. Spread each layer with the frosting, stacking them as you go. Then frost the sides. To set the frosting, refrigerate the cake for 20 minutes before serving.

Yield: One 9 inch, 4 layer cake

BUNDT CAKE

JUNE SCHWARCZ

Cake:
¾ cup butter, plus 1 tablespoon butter, softened
1½ cups sugar
3 eggs, separated
3 cups cake flour
1½ teaspoons baking powder
1 teaspoon baking soda
1½ cups buttermilk
2 teaspoons grated orange rind
½ teaspoon almond extract
1½ teaspoons vanilla extract
2 tablespoons flour

Glaze:
½ cup strained fresh orange juice
½ cup sugar

In a large bowl, cream ¾ cup of the butter and the sugar together until they are light and fluffy. Add the egg yolks, one at a time, beating well after each addition.

Sift together the cake flour, baking powder and baking soda, then add these dry ingredients alternately with the buttermilk to the butter-and-sugar mixture, combining them thoroughly. Flavor the batter with the orange rind and the almond and vanilla extracts.

In another bowl, beat the egg whites until they are stiff, then fold them gently but thoroughly into the batter. Grease a cast-iron Bundt cake mold with the remaining tablespoon of butter, then dust it with the 2 tablespoons of flour, knocking out any excess. Pour the batter into the mold and bake in a preheated 350° oven for 50 minutes, or until a knife inserted in the center of the cake comes out clean.

Cool the cake in its mold, then invert it onto a cake platter. It should slide out easily.

Meanwhile, prepare the glaze: Boil the orange juice and sugar in a small saucepan, stirring frequently, for 3 to 4 minutes. While it is still hot, brush the glaze onto the cake with a pastry brush.

Yield: One 10 inch Bundt cake

TORT' ANTELLA

ELIZABETH WOODMAN

Cake:
 3 teaspoons butter, softened, plus ½ cup butter, softened
 3 teaspoons flour
 ½ cup confectioners' sugar
 4 eggs, separated
 1 cup cake flour
 1 teaspoon baking powder
 ½ teaspoon salt
 3 tablespoons milk
1½ teaspoons vanilla
 ½ teaspoon cream of tartar
 1 cup sugar
 1 teaspoon cider vinegar
 ½ cup slivered almonds

Filling:
 1 cup heavy cream
 1 cup yoghurt (unflavored)
 1 pint strawberries, washed, hulled and halved, or
     1 pint other fresh berries

Grease each of three 8-inch round cake pans with 1 teaspoon of the butter, then dust each with 1 teaspoon of flour, knocking any excess flour from the pans.

To make the cake: With a rotary or electric mixer, beat the ½ cup softened butter in a bowl until it is light and fluffy. Gradually, add the confectioners' sugar, then the egg yolks, one at a time, beating constantly. Combine the cake flour, baking powder and salt and sift them together twice. Add the sifted ingredients to the butter-and-egg mixture, alternating them with the milk, and beating until they are smooth. Stir in ½ teaspoon of the vanilla. Divide the batter evenly among the 3 prepared cake pans.

In another bowl, combine the egg whites with the cream of tartar and beat until the egg whites are stiff. Gradually add the sugar and continue to beat until the whites stand up in stiff peaks. Beat in the cider vinegar and the remaining teaspoon of vanilla. Then, divide the meringue among the three cake pans, smoothing it with a rubber spatula evenly over the batter. Sprinkle ⅓ of the slivered almonds over each pan. Then, bake the layers in a preheated 325° oven for 30 minutes. Carefully remove the layers from the pans, and cool them, almond side up, on wire racks.

To make the filling: Beat the cream until it is stiff. Gently fold the yoghurt into the cream, mixing to blend the two thoroughly. Spread ½ this mixture on each of two cake layers. Then scatter ½ the strawberries on each of the two layers. Stack these two layers on each other, and top them with the third layer. Serve immediately.

Yield: One 3 layer torte

CHRISTMAS FRUITCAKE SQUARES

MAX LENDERMAN

1 teaspoon butter, softened
1 teaspoon flour, plus 2 cups flour
1 cup dried apricots, cut into ¼-inch pieces
1 cup drained, peeled, pitted and coarsely chopped
    canned plums, with their liquid reserved
1 cup seedless raisins
1 cup drained, peeled, pitted and coarsely chopped
    canned apricots
1 cup pitted dates, cut in half lengthwise
1 cup coarsely chopped pecans
½ cup salad oil
1⅔ cups sugar
3 eggs
1¼ teaspoons baking soda
1 teaspoon ground nutmeg
1 teaspoon ground cinnamon
¼ teaspoon ground cloves
1 teaspoon salt

Crumb Topping:
3 tablespoons flour
¾ cup sugar
3 tablespoons butter
½ cup pecan halves
½ cup candied cherries
    Confectioners' sugar

Grease a 13-by-9-by-2-inch baking pan with the teaspoon of butter and dust it with the teaspoon of flour,
knocking the excess flour from the pan.

In a large bowl, combine the dried apricots, plums, raisins, canned apricots, dates and pecans. Toss the fruits to
mix them, then set the bowl aside. Set ⅔ cup of the reserved plum liquid aside and discard the remainder.

In another large bowl, thoroughly combine the oil
and sugar, then add the eggs, one at a time, beating well
after each addition. Combine and sift the 2 cups of flour
with the baking soda, nutmeg, cinnamon, cloves and salt.
Add the dry ingredients alternately with the reserved
⅔ cup of plum liquid to the batter and mix until the
batter is smooth. Drop in the reserved fruits and blend
gently. Pour the batter into the prepared baking pan.

To make the topping: Combine the flour and sugar
and, with two knives or your finger tips, cut the butter into the mixture until it resembles coarse meal.
Then scatter the topping over the batter in the baking pan.

165

Finally, arrange the pecan halves and candied cherries decoratively over the topping. Bake in a preheated 350° oven for 1½ hours, or until a knife inserted in the center of the fruitcake comes out almost clean. Because the fruit is moist, some liquid will adhere to the knife. Cool the cake in the pan, then sprinkle it generously with the confectioners' sugar and cut it into 1½-inch squares.

Yield: Twenty-eight 1½ inch squares

CHOCOLATE SILK PIE

JEAN DELIUS

½ cup butter, softened
¾ cup confectioners' sugar
3 ounces unsweetened chocolate, melted
2 eggs
One 7 inch prebaked pie shell
¾ cup heavy cream

With an electric mixer, beat the butter at medium speed for 5 minutes. (To guarantee the success of this recipe, you must not stint on the time spent beating in the various ingredients.) Gradually add the sugar and beat 5 minutes. Next, add the melted chocolate, and beat 5 minutes longer. Finally, add the eggs, one at a time, beating 5 minutes after each addition.

Pour the mixture into the prebaked pie shell and chill for at least 2 hours. Just before serving, whip the cream and, with a pastry tube or spatula, cover the surface of the pie. Serve cold.

Serves 8.

CHOCOLATE ANGEL PIE

MARY NYBURG

Shell:
- ½ teaspoon butter
- 2 egg whites
- ⅛ teaspoon salt
- ⅛ teaspoon cream of tartar
- ½ cup sugar
- ½ teaspoon vanilla
- ½ cup finely chopped pecans

Filling:
- ¼ pound sweet chocolate
- 3 tablespoons hot water
- ¼ cup orange juice
- 2 teaspoons grated orange rind
- 1 cup heavy cream

To make the shell: Grease an 8-inch pie plate with the butter. In a medium-sized bowl, beat the egg whites, salt and cream of tartar until the egg whites begin to stiffen. Very gradually add the sugar and continue to beat until the whites form stiff peaks. Beat in the vanilla and then, as gently as possible, fold in the pecans. Pile the meringue into the prepared pie plate and, with a rubber spatula, swirl the mixture up the sides of the pie plate and flatten down the center to form a pie-shaped meringue shell. Bake in a preheated 275° oven for 1 hour. Remove from the oven and cool.

To make the filling: Combine the chocolate, hot water, orange juice and orange rind in a double boiler and cook, stirring frequently, over boiling water. When the chocolate has melted and the ingredients are thoroughly blended, remove the mixture from the heat and set aside to cool.

Meanwhile, beat the cream until it is stiff. Gently fold the cooled chocolate mixture into it, then pour the filling into the meringue shell, spreading it evenly. Refrigerate until the pie is served. However, it is best not to prepare this dessert too far in advance, or the shell will become soggy.

Serves 6.

FRESH PEACH PIE

FRANCES ROBINSON

One 9 inch unbaked pie shell

Filling:
½ cup sugar
2 tablespoons cornstarch
¼ cup water
¼ to ½ cup light corn syrup, depending on the sweetness of the peaches
4 cups peeled and sliced peaches
1 tablespoon lemon juice

Topping:
6 tablespoons sugar
¼ cup flour
2 tablespoons butter, softened
1 teaspoon finely grated lemon rind
Whipped cream (optional)

Line the unbaked pie shell with aluminum foil. In the center, place a mound of uncooked rice or dried beans. Bake the shell in a preheated 425° oven for 10 minutes. Remove the foil and rice or beans, reduce the oven temperature to 350° and bake 15 minutes longer. Set aside to cool.

Meanwhile, make the filling: Combine the sugar and cornstarch and gradually pour in the water, stirring constantly over low heat until they form a smooth paste. Add the corn syrup, blend well, then add the sliced peaches. Raise the heat, bring the liquid to a boil and continue to boil for 1 minute. Remove from the heat and cool. Stir in the lemon juice.

While the peaches are cooling, make the topping: Blend the sugar and flour and cut the butter into it until the mixture resembles coarse meal. Sprinkle in the lemon rind and mix well.

To assemble the pie: Pour the filling into the cooked shell, distribute the topping evenly over the peaches and bake in a preheated 425° oven for 25 to 30 minutes. Serve with the whipped cream, if you are using it.

Serves 8.

CHERRY BAVARIAN CREAM PIE

PHYLLIS YACOPINO

Granola crust:
1½ cups granola
 ¼ cup dark brown sugar
 6 tablespoons butter, melted
 1 teaspoon cinnamon

Filling:
 1 envelope unflavored gelatine
 ½ cup sugar
 ⅛ teaspoon salt
 2 eggs, separated
1¼ cups milk
1½ cups fresh cherries, pitted, or substitute 1½ cups
        unsweetened canned cherries, pitted
 ½ teaspoon vanilla
 1 cup heavy cream

To make the crust: Combine the granola, brown sugar, melted butter and cinnamon and mix well. Press the mixture into a 10-inch pie plate, spreading it evenly over the surface and sides. Bake in a preheated 300° oven for 15 minutes, then cool and refrigerate.

To make the filling: Combine the gelatine, ¼ cup of the sugar and the salt in the top of a double boiler. Beat the egg yolks with the milk and add them to the gelatine mixture. Stir over boiling water 5 minutes. Cool, then refrigerate the mixture until it is the consistency of mayonnaise.

Meanwhile, select ten of the more perfect cherries and cut them in half, then reserve them. Coarsely chop the remaining cherries and set them aside.

When the gelatine mixture has thickened, beat the egg whites until they are stiff. Slowly add the remaining ¼ cup of sugar and continue to beat until the whites stand in strong peaks. Flavor with the vanilla. In another bowl, beat the cream until it too is stiff.

Fold the gelatine mixture into the egg whites, then gently blend in the whipped cream. Add the chopped cherries. Spoon the Bavarian cream filling into the granola crust, peaking and swirling the mixture. Decorate the surface with the reserved cherry halves. Refrigerate to set the filling, then serve the pie chilled.

Serves 8 to 10.

RUSSIAN CREAM

LAURE SCHOENFELD

32 lady fingers
8 tablespoons medium-dark rum
¼ cup seedless raspberry preserves
2 cups heavy cream
2 egg yolks
1 cup sugar

Split the lady fingers in half. Sprinkle the halves with 5 tablespoons of the rum. Spread each half with raspberry preserves, then, sandwich-fashion, close them again. Arrange them vertically in concentric circles beginning at the outside edge of an 8-inch soufflé dish.

In a mixing bowl, beat the cream until it is stiff. Then, in a larger bowl, beat the egg yolks for 2 to 3 minutes until they are light and lemon-colored. Gradually add the sugar and continue to beat for several minutes. Pour in the remaining 3 tablespoons of rum and beat to incorporate it thoroughly. Pour about ¼ of the whipped cream into the egg mixture to lighten it, then fold it back into the remaining whipped cream, and mix until it is just blended. Pour the mixture over the lady fingers. Refrigerate for at least 3 hours, or until thoroughly chilled.

Serves 8.

CRUNCHY CHOCOLATE BUTTERCREAM

JON B. WAHLING

2 cups crushed vanilla wafers (about 50), or 1 cup crushed vanilla wafers combined with 1 cup finely chopped walnuts
½ cup butter, softened
1 cup confectioners' sugar
3 eggs, separated
1½ ounces unsweetened chocolate, melted

Scatter a ¼ inch layer of the crushed vanilla wafers, or the wafer-walnut combination, over the bottom of a 9-by-12-inch baking dish. Use about 1½ cups of the wafers and reserve the remaining ½ cup.

In a medium-sized bowl, cream the butter until it is very light and fluffy. Add the sugar and the egg yolks, beating constantly. Blend in the melted chocolate.

In a separate bowl, beat the egg whites until they are stiff, then fold them into the butter-chocolate mixture, mixing them thoroughly. (They may not combine completely.) Spoon the mixture over the crushed wafers in the pan and sprinkle the remaining cup of wafers over the top. Refrigerate for at least 3 hours. Serve chilled.

Serves 8 to 10.

PUNJAB PUDDING

NORMA WESLEY

2 cups Half-and-Half
½ cup date sugar (available at health-food stores)
3 eggs
½ cup unsweetened shredded coconut (available at
    health-food stores)
1 teaspoon vanilla
1 teaspoon butter

Sauce:
½ cup water
½ cup honey
¼ cup coarsely chopped walnuts
2 tablespoons lemon juice

In a small saucepan combine the Half-and-Half and the date sugar. Warm the mixture over low heat, stirring constantly to dissolve the date sugar as much as possible. (It won't dissolve completely.)

Place the eggs in an electric blender, cover and blend for 10 seconds. When the Half-and-Half mixture has come to a scald, add it, the shredded coconut and the vanilla to the eggs. Cover and blend for another 10 seconds. Grease individual baking cups or a 1-quart soufflé dish with the teaspoon of butter and pour in the blender contents. Set the cups or dish in a pan of boiling water and bake in a preheated 350° oven for 20 to 25 minutes for the individual cups and 30 to 40 minutes for the soufflé dish, or until a knife inserted in the center of the pudding comes out clean.

Remove the cups or dish from the pan of water, cool the pudding, and then refrigerate.

To make the sauce: In a small saucepan combine the water, honey and walnuts and bring to a boil. Continue to boil over medium heat for 5 to 10 minutes, or until the syrup has been reduced by half. Stir occasionally, being careful that the mixture doesn't boil over. Lower the heat if necessary. Remove from the stove and stir in the lemon juice. Cool the sauce, then pour it over the pudding.

Serves 6 to 8.

LEMON PUDDING-CAKE

MICHAEL ARNTZ

3 tablespoons butter
1½ cups sugar
4 eggs, separated
6 tablespoons flour
⅛ teaspoon salt
2 cups milk, scalded
⅔ cups lemon juice

In a medium-sized bowl, cream the butter until it is light and fluffy. Gradually add the sugar and continue to beat the mixture until it has the consistency of coarse meal. Drop in the egg yolks, one at a time, beating well after each addition. Combine the flour and salt and add them alternately with the scalded milk, blending until the mixture is smooth. Finally, mix in the lemon juice.

In a separate bowl, beat the egg whites until they are very stiff. Fold them gently into the egg yolk mixture, incorporating them thoroughly. Pour the custard into a 10-inch round oven-proof baking dish. The egg whites will rise to the surface, so that when the pudding-cake is baked, the top will be a light sponge cake covering a soft, smooth lemon pudding.

Set the baking dish in a pan of boiling water so that the water reaches halfway up the sides of the dish. Bake in a preheated 325° oven for 45 to 60 minutes or until a knife inserted in the center of the pudding-cake comes out clean.

Serves 6 to 8.

Editors' comments: *If you prefer to serve the pudding-cake in individual custard dishes, reduce the baking time to 25 to 30 minutes.*

STEAMED CARROT PUDDING

FRANCES ROBINSON

1 cup peeled and finely grated raw potatoes
1 cup scraped and finely grated raw carrots
1 teaspoon baking soda
1 cup sugar
1 cup flour
1 teaspoon salt
1 tablespoon cinnamon
½ cup butter, melted, plus 1 teaspoon butter, softened
1 cup raisins or currants

Set the raw potatoes and carrots into a sieve, pressing them hard to release their liquid. Then transfer them to a bowl. Sift together the baking soda, sugar, flour, salt and cinnamon and stir them into the grated vegetables. Add the melted butter and mix well to incorporate it into the batter. Finally, fold in the raisins or currants, stirring to distribute them evenly.

Grease a 1-quart pudding mold with the remaining teaspoon of butter. Pour the carrot mixture into the mold, then cover it with heavy duty aluminum foil and tie it securely in place. Place the mold in a steamer, add boiling water to within 1 inch of the top of the mold, cover the steamer and steam for 2½ hours, adding more boiling water if necessary.

To serve, slide a knife around the edge of the pudding. Place a serving platter over the mold, invert platter and mold, shake, and the pudding should slide out easily. Serve with hard sauce while the pudding is steaming hot.

Serves 6 to 8.

Editors' comments: *If you do not own a steamer, here is an improvisation: Remove the top and bottom lids of a 1¾-inch high can, and place the can in the bottom of a Dutch Oven or 8- to 10-quart pot. Position the pudding mold so that it rests on the can rim, fill the pot with water, and proceed as above.*

SEMOLINA PUDDING

FRANCES FELTEN

¼ cup butter
1 cup semolina, or quick-cooking Cream of Wheat
½ cup sugar
2 cups milk
½ teaspoon ground cardamom
¼ cup slivered almonds
2 teaspoons shelled and coarsely chopped pistachio nuts
1 cup heavy cream

In a 2- to 3-quart saucepan, melt the butter, add the semolina and stir until the cereal has absorbed all of the melted butter. Continue to cook over low heat, stirring frequently, until the mixture is slightly toasted and golden brown. Add the sugar, then gradually pour in the milk, stirring constantly to keep the mixture smooth. Add the cardamom, almonds and pistachio nuts and continue to cook over low heat, stirring frequently, until the mixture is thick.

This pudding can be served hot, with pouring or whipped cream. Or it can be poured into an 8-inch square cake pan, cooled, cut into squares and served with the pouring or whipped cream.

Serves 6 to 8.

FRESH 'SPIKED' FRUIT SALAD

CYNTHIA SCHIRA

2 oranges, peeled and sectioned
2 or 3 ripe peaches, peeled and sliced
½ honeydew melon, cut into balls
    One 20-ounce can pineapple sections, in heavy syrup
1 pint fresh raspberries, or two 10-ounce boxes frozen raspberries
    Sugar to taste
¼ cup orange liqueur, such as Cointreau or Grand Marnier

In a ceramic or glass serving bowl, combine the fruit and berries and toss gently to mix them. Taste the fruit before adding the sugar, then sweeten to taste with the sugar or with a combination of sugar and pineapple syrup. Pour in the orange liqueur and chill before serving.

Serves 4 to 6.

Editors' comments: *Fruit salad can be made with any combination of fruits—the fresher the better. However, it is a good idea to include as a base one particularly juicy fruit, such as oranges. If you use bananas, add them at the last minute, so that they will not turn brown and diminish the dessert's eye-appeal. Allow about ¾ cup mixed fruit and 1 tablespoon orange liqueur per serving.*

DANISH OAT COOKIES
HANS CHRISTENSEN

2 eggs
1 cup sugar
1 cup butter, melted, plus 1 teaspoon butter, softened
1 teaspoon molasses
¼ teaspoon salt
¼ teaspoon cinnamon (optional)
5 cups "quick" oatmeal
¼ cup water

In a medium-sized bowl, beat the eggs until they are light and frothy. Beating constantly, gradually pour in the sugar, melted butter, molasses, salt and the cinnamon if you are using it. When the mixture is thoroughly blended, stir in the oatmeal. Add the water and if the batter is still a little dry pour in an additional tablespoon or two of water.

Grease a 16-by-11-by-1-inch pan with the remaining teaspoon of butter and spread the batter in it, smoothing it into the corners with a rubber spatula. Bake in a preheated 350° oven for 30 minutes, or until the top is delicately golden.

Immediately cut into squares or triangles, but do not remove the cookies from the pan until they are cool.

Yield: About 36 cookies

GRANOLA RAISIN COOKIES

JODY KLEIN

1 teaspoon butter, softened, plus ½ cup butter, softened
½ cup sugar
½ cup dark brown sugar
1 egg
1 cup flour
½ teaspoon baking powder
½ teaspoon baking soda
½ teaspoon salt
½ cup powdered Tiger's Milk
1 tablespoon milk
1 teaspoon vanilla
1½ cups granola
½ cup seedless raisins

Grease a cookie sheet with the teaspoon of softened butter.

In a large bowl, beat the remaining ½ cup butter until it is light and fluffy. Gradually add the sugar and the dark brown sugar, beating well after each addition. Then add the egg and mix thoroughly.

Sift together the flour, baking powder, baking soda and salt, and add them to the butter-and-sugar mixture. Beat in the Tiger's Milk, milk and vanilla. Finally, add the granola and raisins and mix until they are thoroughly incorporated.

Drop the batter by the teaspoonful onto the prepared cookie sheet. Bake the cookies for 10 to 12 minutes in a preheated 350° oven, until the cookies are golden brown.

Yield: 3 dozen cookies

BIOGRAPHIES OF THE CRAFTSMEN

Sally Adams *(Atlanta, Georgia)* co-founded The Signature Shop in Atlanta which has promoted crafts since 1963. She was an accomplished weaver, a former trustee of the American Crafts Council, and member of the Georgia Commission on the Arts. Mrs. Adams died this June while our book was being assembled.
Katy's Summer Soup P. 21

Adela Akers *(Philadelphia, Pennsylvania)* has a peripatetic background: born in Spain, she spent her childhood in Cuba and attended the University of Havana before coming to the U.S. in 1957. She has worked with weavers in Peru and Mexico and was a resident craftsman at the Penland School of Crafts before setting up a studio in New Jersey. She now teaches weaving at Tyler School of Art, Temple University.
Herbed Rice P. 123
Curried Cranberry-Walnut Relish P. 130

Ray Allen *(Verona, Wisconsin)* is among a younger group of ceramists whose work is sharply observant and often critical of the spirit of contemporary life. He was a featured craftsman in the Museum of Contemporary Crafts exhibition "Clayworks: 20 Americans." He has taught ceramics at the University of Cincinnati and is now Director of the Madison Art Center School.
Hungarian Spaghetti P. 62

Michael Arntz *(Santa Barbara, California)* was a recipient of an American Crafts Council "Young Americans" fellowship in 1970. He has been exploring and teaching ceramics since 1964 when he received a master's degree from California State College at Long Beach. His work, which includes large-scale forms as well as wheel-thrown vessels, was shown most recently in the exhibition "International Ceramics 1972" at the Victoria and Albert Museum, London.
Lemon Pudding-Cake P. 174

Ralph Bacerra *(Los Angeles, California)* is a graduate of the Chouinard Art School in Los Angeles where until 1972 he was chairman of the ceramics department. His work appeared in the Museum of Contemporary Crafts exhibition "Salt Glaze Ceramics" and is in the permanent collection of the Museum of Modern Art in Kyoto, Japan, a country he is visiting on an extended foreign tour.
Adobo Baboy P. 53

Clayton Bailey *(Crockett, California)* was graduated from the University of Wisconsin in 1962 and received a Tiffany Foundation grant a year later. He works in clay but also has made "rubber grubs" and miscellaneous objects. His much exhibited clay critters were seen in "Clayworks: 20 Americans" at the Museum of Contemporary Crafts and earlier his clay nose cups appeared in "Coffee, Tea & Other Cups" also at the Museum. His latest interests are paleontological, though clay-related.
Chile Con Queso P. 102

Harris Barron *(Brookline, Massachusetts)* and his wife Ros, were among the first craftsmen to have their work exhibited in the early years of the Museum of Contemporary Crafts. Their one-man exhibition in 1960 featured ceramic reliefs which the Barrons designed and for which they received numerous commissions in ensuing years. In 1972 they produced and directed Kandinsky's "The Yellow Sound" at New York's Guggenheim Museum as part of a company called "Zone, Theater of the Visual."
"Ooshiwalla" Crab Soup P. 23

Jamie Bennett *(New Paltz, New York)* is completing his MFA studies in gold and silversmithing at New York State College, New Paltz where he is also a teaching assistant. Though a very young craftsman, his work has been shown in exhibitions including the University of Georgia Invitational Student Metal Exhibiton, and, in 1972, at the Fairtree Gallery in New York.
Chicken Cutlet Alla Grippi P. 79
Chicken Oreganato P. 79
"Mixed Media" Salad P. 137

Helen Bitar's *(Portland, Oregon)* thickly embroidered, sun-colored pillows have appeared in many exhibitions. She is also proficient in macrame and has taught a variety of textile crafts at the University of Montana and at New York's New School. She returned to the west in 1972 and is living in Oregon.
Lamb Curry P. 44

Cynthia Bringle *(Penland, North Carolina)* set out to be a full-time craftsman as soon as she graduated from Alfred University in 1964. She is today one of a small number of women who make their living from the production of functional pottery. A frequent workshop leader and often seen at craft fairs in the south, she was elected in 1971 as a trustee of the American Crafts Council.
Easy Oatmeal Bread P. 26

Eleen Auvil Brogan *(Convent Station, New Jersey)* has had an extensive career as a weaver and textile designer. Many of her rug designs, with their rhythmical use of high and low pile and soft color harmonies, have been produced by industry. For several years a resident of Detroit, in 1972 she moved east into a large Victorian home which is fast reflecting her design talent.
Stuffed Leg of Lamb P. 48
Steamed "Kamada" Squash P. 115

Jane Brown *(Penland, North Carolina)* has planned and cooked hundreds of meals for students who have attended the respected Penland School of Crafts where her husband Bill Brown is director. Besides her involvement with the school and her family, she is deeply interested in dyslexic children to whom she gives instruction.
Stifado P. 62
Carrot Cake P. 147

Myra Buchner *(Florham Park, New Jersey)* together with her husband Stan has been much involved in the formation and activities of the New Jersey Designer Craftsmen organization. Her specialty is stitchery which she teaches at the Montclair Art

Museum and Morris Museum in New Jersey.
Spinach Salad P. 142
Cheesecake P. 148

Anna Kang Burgess *(Carmel, California)* was born
and educated in Hawaii and later attended Cranbrook Academy of Art. Her hanging constructions
and weavings have been shown in major exhibitions, but in the last few years much of her time
has been devoted to Origins, a craft shop she and
her husband operated in Carmel until 1972. She
now devotes full time to weaving.
Pul Kogi (Korean Barbecued Meat) P. 63
Kaji Chon (Korean Fried Eggplant) P. 110
Toasted Sesame Seeds P. 134

Mary Balzer Buskirk *(Monterey, California)* took a
year's leave from weaving when she accompanied
her husband on sabbatical to Germany in 1971.
Prior to this she had exhibited her weavings at the
Henry Gallery, University of Washington and at
the Studio Weavers Gallery in Monterey. Her work
is in the collection of the San Diego Fine Arts Gallery and in 1972 Bethel College in Kansas held a
solo exhibition of her weavings.
Always Rare Roast Beef P. 68

Hans Christensen *(Rochester, New York)* has a mas-
tery of metalcraft acquired in his native Denmark.
He worked for several years for Georg Jensen
Silversmiths in Copenhagen prior to coming to the
U.S. in 1954 to join the faculty of the School for
American Craftsmen, Rochester Institute of Tech-
nology, where he teaches metalsmithing. His work
was most recently exhibited in "Radial 80" spon-
sored by the Xerox Corporation.
Frikadeller (Swedish Meatballs) P. 58
Danish Oat Cookies P. 178

Marian Clayden *(Los Gatos, California)* was born
in England where she trained as a painter. For the
last six years as a full-time craftsman she has spe-
cialized in the tritik technique of textile printing.
Her gift for color was seen in the Museum of Contemporary Crafts exhibition "Fabric Vibrations."
Fabrics she has designed have been used in seven
different stagings of the musical "Hair" and in other
theatrical productions.
Boeuf Bretonne P. 64

Herbert Cohen *(Charlotte, North Carolina)* studied
to be a ceramist at Alfred University, but since 1959
he has been with the Mint Museum of Art where
he is director of exhibits. He initiated the Museum's
southeastern regional craft exhibition which is held
annually. Currently he is building a new home and
studio in the North Carolina mountains where he
expects to resume his ceramic interests.
Baked Rice P. 124
Sambumbia Cake with Pudding Sauce P. 150

Margret Craver *(Boston, Massachusetts)* has
taught, filmed, and written about the craft of silversmithing for many years. She is a consultant to
the Museum of Fine Arts in Boston and a research-
er in metal techniques; the sixteenth-century pro-

cess of en resille enameling is a special interest.
Baked Cardamom Carrots P. 108

W. Ron Crosier *(Beaverton, Oregon)* studied
weaving at the University of Oregon and Cranbrook Academy of Art. In 1972 he was awarded a
one-man exhibition at the Henry Gallery, University of Washington where he exhibited large all-
white transparent weavings. He teaches art and
weaving at Adams High School, an experimental
school.
Cabbage and Carrot Borscht P. 71

Jean Delius *(Buffalo, New York)* has had a long as-
sociation with craft activities in New York State as
metalsmith, university professor, and events-organizer.
She was elected in 1971 as a trustee of the
American Crafts Council and is on the faculty of
New York State College, Oswego.
Chocolate Silk Pie P. 167

Robert Ebendorf *(Highland, New York)* collects mem-
orabilia like tin boxes, toys, and photographs. He
reveals his bent for mechanics and detail in his
own fabricated jewelry and objects which were in a
one-man exhibition in 1972 at the Craft Alliance
Gallery in St. Louis. On the faculty of the State
University College, New Paltz, he is also vice-presi-
dent of the Society of North American Goldsmiths.
"Chinese" Turkey P. 77

Shirley Eck *(Muncy, Pennsylvania)* became interested
in weaving through her dentist husband John who
joins her in the production of colorful yardage and
wall hangings. They share not only weaving interests but give much time to such organizations
as the American Crafts Council to which they have
been state representatives for a number of years.
They are chairmen of the 1973 Northeast Crafts
Fair sponsored by the Council.
Honey-Yoghurt Bread P. 27
Timberline Beef Stew P. 66.

Fred Escher *(Janesville, Wisconsin)* has been teaching design and sculpture since 1967 when he received an MFA degree from the University of Wis-
cousin. He is also a filmmaker—one of his films is apt-
ly named "Eating Dinner"—and the author of
"Hiding," a book of photographs. He is chairman
of the art department of Milton College.
Refrigerator Rolls P. 30
Cheese Torte P. 149
Fresh Apple Cake P. 152

Allen Fannin *(Brooklyn, New York)* is a weaver and
spinner as well as an author—of "Handspinning:
Art and Technique" published in 1970. Together
with his wife Dorothy he often demonstrates the art
of handspinning and gives private weaving instruction at his studio. Woven hangings of hand-spun
yarns by them have been shown in numerous exhibitions including a group show in 1972 at The
Studio Museum in Harlem.
Pork Kidneys with Onions P. 56

Frances Felten *(Winsted, Connecticut)* is one of
the few present-day masters of pewtersmithing
which she has been practicing full time since 1934.

Nearly all of her work is by commission. Each year she demonstrates her skill with pewter at the Guilford Handcrafts Exposition held in summer on-the-green in Guilford, Connecticut. She also participates in the Society of Connecticut Craftsmen.
Semolina Pudding P. 176

Arline Fisch *(San Diego, California)* is both a weaver and metalsmith but it is as the latter that she has gained international recognition for her silver jewelry and objects. In 1971 she received a gold medal award in the exhibition "Form and Quality" at the International Handicrafts Fair, Munich. In the same year she was given a solo exhibition at Goldsmiths' Hall, London. She is a trustee of the American Crafts Council and professor of art at San Diego State College.
Spinach and Orange Salad P. 141

Ruth Ginsberg-Place *(South Dartmouth, Massachusetts)* was until 1972 an assistant professor at Southern Illinois University where she taught weaving. She also did textile research in South America while associated with the University. Now, as a full-time craftsman she is involved with architectural commissions and gives occasional workshops. Her tapestries—"Woven Monoliths"—were exhibited most recently at Craft Alliance Gallery, St. Louis.
Chilled Yoghurt-Cucumber Soup P. 19
Lamb-Stuffed Eggplant P. 46
Sylvia's Apple Cake P. 153

Wilhelmina Godfrey *(Buffalo, New York)* is a weaver and Director of Creative Crafts at the Langston Hughes Center for the Visual & Performing Arts in Buffalo. Her weavings were shown in a number of invitational exhibitions during 1972, among them "Radial 80" at the Xerox Corporation and at Buffalo State College during their women's symposium. She is a member of New York State Craftsmen and has participated in their annual fair at Ithaca College for several summers.
Bouillabaisse P. 89
Chinese Chicken and Tomatoes P. 80
Red Beans and Rice P. 122

Paula Gollhardt *(Summit, New Jersey)* works in metal and textiles with equal aplomb. She likes to travel—in summer to craft fairs where she sells her jewelry and colorful felt dolls, and to a country place in Vermont which she is gradually remodeling. Active with New Jersey Designer Craftsmen, she is also a state representative to the American Crafts Council.
Indonesian Lamb Sate P. 47
Picadillo Cubano P. 59
Pilaf P. 126

Gwen-Lin Goo *(Shaker Heights, Ohio)* has experimented with double-and triple-layered silk-screened hangings which have been shown in major exhibitions including the American Crafts Council "Young Americans" competition. She is equally proficient in ceramics. Born in Hawaii and trained at the School of The Art Institute of Chicago and Cranbrook Academy of Art, she currently teaches textile printing at the Cleveland Institute of Art.
Chinese Beef and Asparagus P. 67

Françoise Grossen *(New York, New York)* was born in Neuchâtel and studied architecture and textile design in Switzerland before doing graduate work at UCLA. Her commissioned complex of knotted rope adorns Chicago's Hyatt House and other of her hangings are part of the Dreyfus Corporation Collection in New York. She was one of thirteen exhibitors in the international exhibition of contemporary fabric forms "Deliberate Entanglements" presented at the UCLA Art Galleries in 1971.
Polish Zucchini P. 138

Trude Guermonprez *(San Francisco, California)* was awarded the Craftmanship Medal of the American Institute of Architects in 1970 for distinguished creative design in weaving. Born and educated abroad, she came to the U.S. during World War II and taught at Black Mountain College and the San Francisco Art Institute. Since 1960 she has been chairman of the crafts department at California College of Arts & Crafts in Oakland where she teaches weaving.
Equality Cake P. 156

Judi Meyers Halem *(Davis, California)* has worked in clay and plastics but is interested in other media as well. She has spent several years at the University of Wisconsin, Madison, where a show of her work—"The Very Soft Core"—was held at the University Galleries in 1972. She recently moved from Madison to a new home in California.
Boiled Brisket of Beef P. 69

Ted Hallman's *(Berkeley, California)* "The Solar Environment," a 12' x 12' pagoda-shaped fabric pavilion of tied and knotted yarns, was recently exhibited in the courtyard of California's Oakland Museum. This is not the first Hallman environment: his woven meditation space appeared in the Museum of Contemporary Crafts exhibition "Contemplation Environments" in 1970. He is teaching weaving at the College of Arts and Crafts in Oakland and at San Jose State College.
Honeyed Carrots with Cashews P. 109

Vivika Heino *(Concord, New Hampshire)* and her husband Otto are studio potters, producing functional stoneware. They have had a long association with crafts, particularly in support of the League of New Hampshire Craftsmen. In 1969 Mrs. Heino worked with the educational television station in New Hampshire to prepare the film "The World and Work of American Craftsmen" which is now being shown abroad. She teaches part-time at New England College.
Buttered Rum Peaches P. 146

Jolyon Hofsted *(Shady, New York)* is director of the Brooklyn Museum Art School where he once studied on a Max Beckmann Scholarship and where he has also taught ceramics. He is the author of "Step-by-Step Ceramics" published in 1967 and of articles in Ceramics Monthly.
Enid's Spareribs P. 57

Ka Kwong Hui *(Jamesburg, New Jersey)* was born in Hong Kong. He came to the U.S. in 1949 and studied pottery with Marguerite Wildenhain and at Alfred University. In 1962 he was awarded a Tiffany Foundation grant and later collaborated with the painter Roy Lichtenstein on a line of ceramic tableware. His brightly glazed ceramic forms are in the collection of the Everson Museum, Syracuse and the Museum of Modern Art, Kyoto, among others. He teaches ceramics at Douglass College, Rutgers University.
Chicken and Corn Soup P. 17

Michael Jerry *(Syracuse, New York)* studied at School for American Craftsmen and Cranbrook Academy of Art. In 1963 he joined the faculty of Stout State University where he developed the design program and introduced studies in metal. His silver jewelry and forged iron have been frequently exhibited, most recently at Shop One in Rochester, and earlier in "Goldsmith '70" at the Minnesota Museum of Art. He has taught at Syracuse University since 1970.
Mike's Potatoes P. 112

John Jessiman *(Cortland, New York)* is an associate professor at the State University College, Cortland where he teaches ceramics. He recently completed a studio in Blodgett Mills, New York where he produces stoneware. His work has been included in the Scripps College Annual and "Art In Other Media" in 1971 at the Burpee Art Museum in Illinois.
Shrimp with Mushrooms P. 91

Karen Karnes *(Stony Point, New York)* has operated a pottery in Stony Point since 1954. She studied ceramics in Italy and at Alfred University and later maintained the pottery shop at Black Mountain College before beginning her own studio. She produces a line of functional salt glaze ceramics as well as special commissioned pieces which have been widely exhibited. Her flame-proof baking dish in which she cooks her chicken recipe is included in the Museum of Contemporary Crafts exhibition "Objects For Preparing Food."
Baked Chicken with Brown Rice P. 81

Bryn Kelsey *(Stony Creek, New York)* designs and sews clothing and dolls which she has sold in her own shop in New York City. She and her potter husband Todd Kelsey are presently remodeling an old resort hotel in Stony Creek as their home and studio.
Peach Chutney P. 131

Ron King *(Penobscot, Maine)* runs a farm in Maine which he started in 1970. Between farming chores he produces a line of woven pillows and rugs which he sells at fairs and shops in the east. His large knitted wall hangings appeared in the Museum of Contemporary Crafts 1972 exhibition "Sculpture in Fiber." He is now completing a commission for a knitted "wall" for the Student Union of Queens College in New York.
Applesauce Cake P. 154

Jody Klein *(Akron, Ohio)* has described herself as a collector and scavenger—of fabrics and things which she assembles into stuffed images using appliqué and fabric patterning techniques. Her latest work is "186 Cascading Hearts," a ten-foot mass of different sized hearts of batiked and embroidered velvet. Her work was included in 1972 in an invitational exhibition of textiles at Ball State College.
Chicken Liver Pâté P. 12
Granola Raisin Cookies P. 179

Howard Kottler *(Seattle, Washington)* wittily applies decals to white porcelain plates which he calls "decal plates." These and other of his works have been included in major exhibitions. He is a craftsman with many degrees, the last being Doctor of Philosophy earned at Ohio State University in 1964. He presently is on the faculty of the University of Washington, Seattle.
Dill Pickles P. 133

Earl Krentzin's *(Grosse Pointe Farms, Michigan)* sculpture is full of personal fantasies masterfully rendered in silver and gold. Machines, bicycles, trains and monster-men, often diminutive, are some of the forms he creates with great detail. A full-time craftsman, his work is represented by the Kennedy Galleries in New York where he has had exhibitions for the past several years.
Lentil Soup P. 22

Ann Krestensen *(Placitas, New Mexico)* became interested in pottery six years ago when she tired of advertising design, her profession since college. In 1972 she opened her own business, Ann Krestensen Pottery, in New Mexico where she produces functional ceramics. She and her husband live in a large adobe house and have just completed an adobe studio as a showplace for Ann's stoneware.
Whole Wheat Bread P. 31
Garden Vegetable Casserole P. 116

Mary Kretsinger *(Emporia, Kansas)* does cloisonné enamel jewelry for which she hammers her own gold wire. Her work is principally done on commission, including church interiors for which she designs a full array of appointments. A four-foot cross she executed in 1968 hangs in the Catholic Chapel of Brandeis University. Aside from a few workshops in enameling each year, she works full time as a craftsman.
Easy Cucumber Soup P. 20

Carolyn Kriegman *(East Orange, New Jersey)* has been making gold and silver jewelry for several years but is also known for her striking neck ornaments in fabricated plastic which were shown in the Museum of Contemporary Crafts exhibition "PLASTIC As Plastic." Carolyn and her husband Sam are devotees of the Maine coast and spend summers in their home on Deer Isle.
Ratatouille Niçoise P. 117

Kara Lang *(Lakewood, Colorado)* is a painter but translates this skill into knitted garments in which she incorporates landscapes and other patterns. Her husband Rodger was a featured craftsman in the Museum of Contemporary Crafts exhibition "Clayworks: 20 Americans." Both did

graduate work at the University of Wisconsin, Madison.
Curried Lamb and Lentils P. 45
Bulgur with Broccoli and Tomatoes P. 119

Ragnhild Langlet *(Sausalito, California)* creates embroidered and appliquéd wall hangings as well as wall sculptures made of shaped and dyed fabric. One of these works covers a 40' wall at Rochester Institute of Technology which commissioned the piece for its new campus in 1969. Born in Sweden and for several years on the faculty of the University of California, Berkeley, she lives and works on a houseboat moored in San Francisco Bay.
Minted Leg of Lamb P. 48
Almond Crusty Cake P. 155

Jack Lenor Larsen *(New York, New York)* is well known as craftsman, designer, and manufacturer of textiles. His place in the field of design has been acknowledged in several one-man exhibitions here and abroad. In 1971 the New York Chapter of A.I.D. presented him the Elsie de Wolfe Award; in 1968 he received the Craftsmanship Medal of the American Institute of Architects. He is also an author, most recently with Mildred Constantine of "Beyond Craft: The Art Fabric." He has long been associated as a trustee with the American Crafts Council and Haystack Mountain School of Crafts.
Dutch Babies P. 38

Bruno LaVerdiere *(Hadley, New York)* was formerly a member of the Benedictine Order and artist-in-residence at St. Martin's Abbey in Washington. A frequent workshop leader in ceramics, he has taught at Greenwich House Pottery in New York and Penland School of Crafts where his wife Sophia studied glassblowing. They and their young son are at Scripps College, California for the remainder of 1972 where Bruno is visiting instructor in ceramics.
Spaghetti Carbonara P. 61

Max Lenderman *(Bowling Green, Ohio)* studied at Indiana State University and at the University of Kansas where he majored in ceramics and weaving. Though he occasionally works in both media, his chief interest is in quadruple weaving; he spoke on this technique recently at the first conference of the Handweavers Guild of America. A one-man exhibition of his work took place at Defiance College in 1972. He has been on the faculty of Bowling Green State University since 1968.
Christmas Fruitcake Squares P. 165

Jennifer Lew *(Seattle, Washington)* is assistant professor of art at the University of Washington, Seattle from which she graduated in 1968. Her printed casement design—"Pinnacle"—selected in the American Crafts Council Competition "Young Americans" is now produced by Jack Lenor Larsen Inc. Most recently she collaborated with the craftsman Richard Proctor on a discharge-dyed quilt shown in "Fabric Vibrations" in 1972 at the Museum of Contemporary Crafts.
Shrimp and Chinese Snow Peas P. 92

Joan Lintault *(San Bernardino, California)* creates stitched and stuffed fabric wall hangings utilizing trapunto technique. These were shown in the "Riverside Fiber Invitational" held in 1972 at the Riverside Art Center. Her work was also included in an exhibition of quilts the same year at The Third Spring Gallery in Washington, D.C. She is proficient with clay as well, having earned an MFA degree in ceramics at Southern Illinois University.
Rose Geranium Pound Cake P. 157

Harvey Littleton *(Verona, Wisconsin)* may be credited with leading the renaissance of the craft of blown glass over the last ten years in the U.S. He studied ceramics at Cranbrook Academy of Art and taught pottery at the University of Wisconsin before a grant from the University in 1962 helped him to establish a glass workshop. Since that period he has taught glassblowing to a score of students and shown his works in major exhibitions here and abroad. His book "Glassblowing: A Search for Form" was published in 1971.
Steamed Stuffed Trout P. 98

Carole Lynne Lubove *(Pittsburgh, Pennsylvania)* specializes in tubular and loom-shaped weavings which were included in the 1972 exhibition of the Pittsburgh Weavers Guild held at the Arts & Crafts Center, Pittsburgh. She takes a non-traditional approach to weaving in courses she teaches at the Center and in workshops she conducts on woven clothing technique. A participant in the activities of several craft groups, she was president of the Craftsmen's Guild of Pittsburgh 1968-70.
Stuffed Grape Leaves P. 10
Quick Cous-Cous P. 88

Warren MacKenzie *(Stillwater, Minnesota)* attended the School of The Art Institute of Chicago and was an apprentice to Bernard Leach at St. Ives, England. He has been teaching ceramics since 1948, nearly twenty of those years as a member of the faculty of the University of Minnesota. He works in stoneware and porcelain, producing utilitarian pottery which he sells through exhibitions or from his studio. He is a member of the National Council on Education for the Ceramic Arts and was a speaker for that group at its Toronto conference in 1971.
Chicken and Wild Rice Casserole P. 85

Sam Maloof *(Alta Loma, California)* was one of five Americans to be featured in "Woodenworks," the inaugural exhibition of the Smithsonian Institution Renwick Gallery in Washington, D.C. in 1972. A self-taught woodworker, he began furniture making in the 40's and has been a full-time craftsman ever since. With the aid of his wife, who manages the business side of affairs, he designs and executes many commissioned pieces annually.
Baked Stuffed Kibbi P. 52
Tabbouleh (Arabic Salad) P. 144

Patrick McCormick *(Bellingham, Washington)* studied at the University of Washington and at Cranbrook Academy of Art on a Ford Foundation grant. His ceramics—non-functional porcelain, frequently incorporating photo silk screen techniques—have been exhibited nationally, most recently in a one-

man exhibition at the Henry Gallery, University of Washington. He lives on a farm in Bellingham and is head of the ceramics department at Western Washington State College.
Never-Fail Chocolate Cake P. 158

Nancy Merritt *(West Chester, Pennsylvania)* is currently completing her master's degree at Tyler School of Art, Temple University. Before entering Tyler she taught weaving at Moore College of Art for five years. Two of her tubular weavings were selected in the American Crafts Council "Young Americans" competition and most recently her tapestries were shown in an exhibition at the DeCordova Museum in Massachusetts.
Marinated Shrimp P. 8
Carrot Soup P. 16

Priscilla Merritt *(Deer Isle, Maine)* runs Centennial House in Deer Isle where she sells crafts made by the faculty of the famous Haystack Mountain School of Crafts which her husband Francis Merritt directs. She added another aspect to Centennial House in 1972 with the opening of a restaurant —Limited Fare—serving organic foods prepared in her warmly decorated kitchen.
Baked Haddock with Lemon Sauce P. 97
Baked Soy Beans P. 121

Eleanor Moty *(Madison, Wisconsin)* studied jewelry and metalsmithing at Tyler School of Art and while there explored photofabrication techniques on metal. Her work employing this process has received recognition in several major exhibitions including "Goldsmith '70" held at the Minnesota Museum of Art. Formerly on the faculty of Moore College of Art, she is now teaching at the University of Wisconsin, Madison.
European Egg Bread P. 29

Mary Stephens Nelson *(Boise, Idaho)* has designed jewelry for a number of years but is interested in textile techniques as well. Her delicate macrame necklaces appeared in the Museum of Contemporary Crafts exhibition "Furs & Feathers" in 1971 and a large crocheted hanging by her was commissioned for the world headquarters of the Boise Cascade Corporation.
Sweet-and-Sour Red Cabbage P. 106

Mike Nevelson *(New Fairfield, Connecticut)* makes large chests of drawers in wood and gives them heads with drawers inside and clock faces or makes them into characters like "Six Conformist Gentlemen." He is a long-time sculptor as well as a lithographer, and has been an artist-in-residence at the Tamarind Institute, a division of the University of New Mexico.
Shrimp Mulligan P. 90

Mary Nyburg *(Garrison, Maryland)* has been making functional pottery since the 50's. Her salt glaze pottery appeared in the Museum of Contemporary Crafts exhibition "Salt Glaze Ceramics" in 1972. She has long been active in craft activities in the northeast—especially the American Crafts Council Northeast Craft Fair—and is presently chairman of the U.S. Section of the World Crafts Council.
Veal Scaloppine with Mushrooms and Cheese P. 74
Chocolate Angel Pie P. 168
Baked Noodles P. 127

Marilyn Pappas *(Miami, Florida)* uses found objects and stitchery to create pictorial hangings such as "Opera Coat" which is in "Objects: USA," the collection of contemporary crafts by American craftsmen assembled in 1969 by the Johnson Wax Company. She was also an exhibitor in "Needle-Art 1972: 7 American Artists" held at the Gimpel and Weitzenhoffer Gallery, New York. Her latest work combines clay elements with stitchery. She is associate professor of art at Miami Dade Junior College.
Madame Renoir's Chicken P. 83
Sauerbraten P. 70
Greek Salad P. 136
Chocolate Chip Nut Cake P. 159

Alice Parrott *(Santa Fe, New Mexico)* was born in Hawaii and studied at Cranbook Academy of Art. Together with her husband Alan Parrott she maintains a production studio where they dye yarns and weave yardage that is sold for interior design projects and at The Market, a shop they operate in Santa Fe. In addition to production weaving, she does individual hangings with dramatic color harmonies that have been included in major exhibitions.
Chinese Roast Duck with Plum Sauce P. 76

Ronald Pearson *(Deer Isle, Maine)* has earned a leading place in crafts for his design and production of gold and silver jewelry. He works in several other metals including forged iron and has done many architectural and private commissions as well as designs for industry. Together with three other craftsmen he founded and still participates in Shop One in Rochester, New York, a major outlet for crafts since 1953.
Sourdough Pancakes P. 42

Maija Woof Peeples *(Folsom, California)* teaches multi-media art at Sierra College in California. Besides painting she works in sculptural crochet and participated in the Oakland Museum exhibition "Sacramento Sampler" in 1972.
Game Hen with Almonds P. 78

Helen Power *(Laramie, Wyoming)* reports that she likes to cook and that is one reason she specializes in ceramic tableware. She has been potting since the 50's in California where she taught at the Arts & Crafts Cooperative in Berkeley, and now in Wyoming in her own studio, Tartarus Workshop.
Beef Charbonnade P. 60

Don Reitz *(Spring Green, Wisconsin)* lives on a rolling farm in Wisconsin where he and his family can indulge their interest in horses and where he is a prolific producer of salt glaze ceramics. His skill and knowledge of technique have made him a popular workshop leader as well as a writer—in the American Crafts Council publication "Salt Glaze Ceramics." He is a professor of art at the University

of Wisconsin, Madison.
Barbecued Fish Steaks P. 96

Frances Robinson *(Mogadore, Ohio)* received a Ford Foundation grant in 1954 for study in Scandinavia where she became interested in stitchery. She refers to her work as sewing-machine tapestries—layers of machine stitching, sometimes pictorial but also abstract. Her stitched panels hang in the Children's Room of the Akron Public Library and an 18' mural was commissioned in 1969 by the Goodyear Bank in Ohio. She retired a few years ago after a career as a high school art teacher.
Fresh Peach Pie P. 169
Steamed Carrot Pudding P. 175

Bill Sax *(South Hadley, Massachusetts)* became a production potter following his study at School for American Craftsmen and apprenticeship with Frans Wildenhain. In 1963 he opened a studio in New Hampshire where he made place settings, casseroles and other stoneware. Now living in Massachusetts, he continues to give full time to his production, selling his work through leading shops in the east. In the summer he grows an invariably splendid vegetable garden.
Baked Brown Rice P. 125

Pat Scarlett *(Palo Alto, California)* studied painting and drawing at the San Francisco Art Institute and ceramics with Ernie Kim. Her work involves painting with glazes on ceramics. Many of these are wall pieces she calls "Ikon Plates" which have been shown at the Anneberg Gallery, San Francisco and in a solo exhibition at Galleria del Sol, Santa Barbara.
Luncheon Mushrooms P. 101

Mary Ann Scherr *(Akron, Ohio)* is on the faculty of Kent State University and has taught for several summers at Penland School of Crafts. She uses stainless steel extensively in her jewelry designs and body ornaments but also works in silver. She received a silver medal, appropriately for a silver gauntlet she designed, in the international exhibition of costume jewelry "Jablonec '71" in Prague.
Danish Cheese Mix P. 13
Egyptian Fathia P. 65
Apple Sauerkraut P. 107

Cynthia Schira *(Lawrence, Kansas)* followed her undergraduate work at Rhode Island School of Design with study of tapestry in Aubusson, France and of printed fabrics at the University of Baroda, India. In 1967 she received a Tiffany Foundation grant after completing a master's degree at the University of Kansas. In 1971 she received one of two purchase awards for a woven aluminum hanging in the exhibition "Women '71" at Northern Illinois University, DeKalb.
"Indian" Fried Fish P. 96
Sauerbraten P. 70
Potato Dumplings P. 113
Fresh "Spiked" Fruit Salad P. 177

Laure Schoenfeld *(Great Neck, New York)* came to the U.S. from Germany in 1943. She became interested in the design of rugs in the late 50's and has been

pursuing this interest ever since. Her hooked rugs of hand-dyed yarns were included in the exhibition "Needle-Art 1972: 7 American Artists" held at the Gimpel and Weitzenhoffer Gallery in New York. She teaches needlepoint and other textile crafts in her own "The City Line Craft Shop" in Little Neck.
Russian Cream P. 171

June Schwarcz *(Sausalito, California)* began enameling as a pastime and has become a recognized craftsman and experimenter in enameling technique. Her work often utilizes a combination of sophisticated processes and has been shown here and in Europe in major exhibitions. She spends full time at her craft, but occasionally gives workshops.
Bundt Cake P. 162
Chocolate Cream Sponge Cake P. 160

Kay Sekimachi *(Berkeley, California)* was one of the first weavers to experiment with synthetic mono-filaments in woven forms. Her graceful work in this material has placed her hangings in numerous exhibitions including the international "Deliberate Entanglements" held at the UCLA Art Galleries in 1971. She teaches at the San Francisco Adult School and in private life is the wife of another well-known craftsman, Bob Stocksdale.
Sunomono (Japanese Cucumber Salad) P. 143

Barbara Shawcroft *(San Anselmo, California)* was born in England where for eight years she was a member of the Royal Academy of Dance, London. She studied ceramics and weaving there prior to coming to the U.S. She is now in graduate studies at the College of Arts & Crafts, Oakland and is experimenting with synthetic yarns and knotless netting techniques. Her crocheted forms appeared in "Sculpture in Fiber" at the Museum of Contemporary Crafts in 1972.
Baked Tomatoes Stuffed with Mushrooms P. 120
Snow Peas, Water Chestnuts and Mushrooms P. 118
Sweet Potatoes with Orange-Rum Glaze P. 114

Wilcke Smith *(Albuquerque, New Mexico)* was much influenced by the innovative stitchery of the late Mariska Karasz in the early 60's and began to teach herself this technique after earlier work in mosaics. She now operates a small studio where she creates colorful wall hangings and gives private stitchery instruction. In 1972 Saint Paul's Lutheran Church in Albuquerque commissioned her to design altar cloths for its new building which has other appointments by southwestern craftsmen.
Seviche P. 9
New Mexican Corn Bread P. 33

Paul Soldner *(Aspen, Colorado)* has a distinguished career as a teacher—at Scripps College in Claremont and in workshops he conducts throughout the United States. He is practiced in many ceramic techniques but is best known for his work in raku and his studies of kiln construction. He was one of nineteen potters to receive an award in the exhibition "International Ceramics 1972" at the Victoria and Albert Museum, London. He is a trustee of the American Crafts Council.

Dilly Casserole Bread P. 32
Fruited Lamb Shanks P. 50
Omelet with Yoghurt and Alfalfa Sprouts P. 100

Mel Someroski *(Penland, North Carolina)* spent several weeks in 1972 as a member of a paramedical team in Nicaragua. He has been drawn to other countries as well, especially Ceylon, where he has operated a workshop with the Dumbara mat weavers. His own weaving, done on and off the loom in grass and hanna fibers, was included in 1972 in the national invitational exhibition of textiles at Ball State College. Presently he is on leave from Kent State University to teach weaving at Penland School of Crafts.
Chicken Buriyani P. 84
Tomato Sambal P. 132

Victor Spinski *(Newark, Delaware)* was a featured craftsman in "Clayworks: 20 Americans" at the Museum of Contemporary Crafts in 1971. His glazed ceramic "machines" are complex takeoffs of industry's own. He is also skilled in the application of photography to clay. Much interested in curriculum, he has researched in this area as a member of the National Council on Education for the Ceramic Arts. He is an assistant professor at the University of Delaware.
Muesli Breakfast Bread P. 39

Jean Stamsta *(Hartland, Wisconsin)* is an instructor in weaving at Alverno College in Milwaukee. She and her husband Duane and two children live in a country school house which they converted with great color into a home and studio. Mrs. Stamsta has exhibited her double woven, stuffed forms in many exhibitions. One of her latest works is called "Jolly Octopus"—a mural-sized tubular weaving commissioned for a residence in Wisconsin.
Basic White Bread P. 34
Breakfast Muffins P. 40
Duane's Pancakes P. 41

Zelda Strecker *(St. Charles, Illinois)* is a prolific creator of screen-printed textiles which she makes into hangings and apparel. She has executed many commissions—textiles for liturgical use and wall murals. Before moving to Illinois in the 60's she taught art in public schools in New York State for nearly twenty years. As a long-time member of New York State Craftsmen, she participates in their annual summer fair at Ithaca College; her textiles are also seen at the Oakbrook Center Invitational Crafts Exhibition in Illinois.
Garlic-Lemon Chicken P. 82

Toshiko Takaezu *(Clinton, New Jersey)* was born in Hawaii and some say her work reflects the quiet drama of that state. She is well known for her ceramics but she is also a weaver of thick and vibrant rya rugs. For several years on the faculty of the Cleveland Institute of Art, she teaches part-time in the Creative Arts Program at Princeton University and maintains a studio in Clinton. She is a busy traveler—to exhibitions of her work across the country—and a juror and workshop leader.
Tempura (Fried Shellfish and Vegetables) P. 93
Pork with Ginger and Soy Sauce P. 55

Byron Temple *(Lambertville, New Jersey)* attended Ball State Teachers College and studied ceramics as an apprentice in the famous Leach Pottery in St. Ives, England. He has been producing a line of functional ceramics in his studio in Lambertville since 1963. Besides his pottery production, he heads the ceramics department at Pratt Institute of Technology, Brooklyn.
Pork with Apricots P. 54

Tom Thomason *(Albuquerque, New Mexico)* a descendent of Oklahoma Cherokees, studied silversmithing with Navajo and Hopi craftsmen before attending the University of New Mexico. In 1962 he opened The Studio Gallery in Old Albuquerque where he sells his own jewelry and holds exhibitions of the work of other craftsmen. He is active in craft events in his state, often showing his work at fairs such as the New Mexico State Fair, where in 1971 he received the purchase prize of the American Institute of Architects.
Guacamole P. 11

Dena Todd *(Houston, Texas)* helped to organize the Houston Designer Craftsmen group in 1968 and remains much involved in their activities. She makes gold and silver jewelry, mostly on commission, and has done so nearly twenty years. Recent exhibitions at the Handmakers Gallery in Houston and the Arkansas Art Center included her metalwork.
Ham in Jellied Herb Sauce P. 101

Louise Todd *(Philadelphia, Pennsylvania)* works with yarns both on and off the loom. Her large woven hanging environment "Under Milkweed" was seen in "Furs & Feathers" in 1971 at the Museum of Contemporary Crafts and in 1970 she created a face veil of fiber optic and nylon fishing line for the Museum's "Face Coverings" exhibition. She studied at Syracuse University and later at Haystack Mountain School of Crafts where she has since taught. She is on the faculty of Moore College of Art, Philadelphia.
Easy Christmas Stollen P. 36

David Van Dommelen *(State College, Pennsylvania)* is the author of several books: "Decorative Wall Hangings," "Walls: Enrichment & Ornamentation," "New Uses For Old Cannon Balls," and the latest, "Designing and Decorating Interiors." In 1972 he travelled in South America on a Ford Foundation grant for crafts research. He does weaving and appliqué which was exhibited recently at Pennsylvania State University where he is a member of the faculty.
Chilled Tomato Soup P. 18

Jon B. Wahling *(Columbus, Ohio)* has been teaching at the Arts and Crafts Center of the Columbus Recreation Department in Ohio since his graduation in 1964 from Cranbrook Academy of Art. He also has taught summer sessions at the Penland School of Crafts. His knotted jute forms were seen in the Museum of Contemporary Crafts "Sculpture in Fiber" exhibition in 1972.
Salade Diable P. 140
Crunchy Chocolate Buttercream P. 172

Phillip Ward *(Gainesville, Florida)* received an MFA degree from Tulane University in 1959 and later was the recipient of a Tiffany Foundation grant for his work in ceramics. Much of this work is in lustre ware and raku. He has been on the faculty of the University of Florida since 1959 and is joined in his interest in ceramics by his wife Jacqueline who is also a potter.
Baked Chicken with Sherry and Grapes P. 82
Braised Red Cabbage with Sausage P. 56

Aileen O. Webb *(New York, New York)* is founder and chairman of the Board of the American Crafts Council. Her interest in crafts has been a long one. She formed a small group called Putnam County Products during the Depression and in 1940 opened America House in New York City for the sale of American Crafts. The establishment of the American Craftsmen's Council followed in 1943; Mrs. Webb was the first editor of its nationally circulated magazine, *Craft Horizons*. She was instrumental in the development of the School for American Craftsmen, now part of Rochester Institute of Technology, and, in 1964, of the World Crafts Council of which she is president. Not least of her accomplishments is that she is a potter.
Quiche Lorraine P. 99

Susan Weitzman's *(New York, New York)* hangings of exposed warp made with wool she hand spins, have been included in such major exhibitions as "Wall Hangings" at the Museum of Modern Art and the International Tapestry Biennale in Lausanne. She also creates miniature tapestries, shown most recently at the Ruth Kaufman Gallery in New York which represents her. She is married to Ephrem Weitzman who is also a craftsman, specializing in architectural commissions.
Raita (Indian Cucumber and Yoghurt Salad) P. 139

Norma Wesley *(Albany, California)* teaches weaving and other textile crafts at the Berkeley Creative Living Center in California. Among many activities, she has participated in the Northern California Handweavers Conference where her weavings have been exhibited.
Punjab Pudding P. 173

Virginia West *(Baltimore, Maryland)* is the author of "Finishing Touches for the Handweaver" published in 1968. She has been active in state and regional craft events and has demonstrated weaving at many of these. Her colorful tapestries were shown in a solo exhibition at the Windbell Gallery in Maryland in 1971. She teaches at Maryland Institute College of Art.
Fresh Peach Cobbler P. 151

Jean J. Williams *(Kaneohe, Hawaii)* was born and educated in Honolulu. Her frequently monumental hangings incorporate native Hawaiian materials, like papaya trunk fibers, along with hand-spun and hand-dyed yarns. She has exhibited her weavings since 1955 and teaches at the University of Hawaii, Honolulu.
No-Knead Cottage Cheese Bread P. 28
Pot Roast, Hawaiian Style P. 73

Paula Winokur *(Horsham, Pennsylvania)* studied at Tyler School of Art where her husband Robert teaches pottery. Together they have run a studio for the production of functional and decorative stoneware. Her work received a jury award in the 9th Annual Southern Tier Arts and Crafts exhibition in 1972 at the Corning Museum of Glass. A solo exhibition of Winokur pottery took place at the Design Corner, Cleveland the same year.
Stir-Fried Steak in Wine. P. 73

Elizabeth Woodman *(Boulder, Colorado)* creates functional stoneware ceramics which are frequently salt glazed. The latter work appeared in the Museum of Contemporary Crafts "Salt Glaze Ceramics" exhibition in 1972; the gnocchi dish in which she prepares the recipe given here is part of the Museum's show "Objects For Preparing Food." She and her painter husband George Woodman spend summers in a house they own in Florence, Italy.
Gnocchi Di Semolino P. 14
Tort'Antella P. 163

Ellamarie Woolley *(San Diego, California)* and her husband, Jackson Woolley, were given a solo exhibition of their work in 1972 at the Museum of Contemporary Crafts. They have been full-time craftsmen for many years and have collaborated on large enamel murals commissioned for several public buildings on the west coast. Since 1966 she has concentrated on smaller and shaped enamels of intense color. These and other of her works are included in collections at the Dallas Museum and the Everson Museum, Syracuse, among others.
Kiln-Baked Potatoes P. 111

William Wyman *(Miami, Florida)* established the Herring Run Pottery in East Weymouth, Massachusetts where he produced functional and sculptural stoneware as well as commissioned works. His ceramics have been much exhibited; one of his slab-formed ceramic sculptures was shown in the exhibition "International Ceramics 1972" at the Victoria and Albert Museum, London. He now teaches ceramics at Florida International University.
Baked Lamb Shanks P. 51
Wyman's Chicken Casserole P. 88

Phyllis Yacopino *(Nyack, New York)* in addition to crafts, has studied dance, a interest which continues to hold her attention. She has been a resident craftsman at Penland School of Crafts where she researched and taught vegetable dyeing and gave yoga instruction as part of the school's Concentration Program. She continues her teaching of vegetable dyeing through special workshops.
Chicken Pilaf with Eggplant P. 86
Cherry Bavarian Cream Pie P. 170

RECIPE INDEX

DESIGNED BY EMIL ANTONUCCI

SET IN 11 POINT PALATINO AND PRINTED
ON MEAD TERRA TEXT AND
CHAMPION CARNIVAL COVER BY
KULKA PRINTING/CAPITAL CITY PRESS
BERLIN, VERMONT